STRANGE AND UNUSUAL MYSTERIES

by The Frightening Floyds

Anubis Press
Louisville, KY

Thank you for reading! If you like the book, please leave a review on Amazon and Goodreads. Reviews help authors and publishers spread the word!

To keep up with more Anubis Press news, join the Anubis Press Dynasty on Facebook.

ALSO BY THE FRIGHTENING FLOYDS:

Louisville's Strange and Unusual Haunts
Kentucky's Haunted Mansions
Haunts of Hollywood Stars and Starlets
Indiana's Strange and Unusual Haunts
Be Our Ghost
Aliens Over Kentucky

ANUBIS PRESS

STRANGE AND UNUSUAL MYSTERIES

by The Frightening Floyds

To Mama

We just wanted to thank you for always giving us wonderful memories. We knew how much you loved *Unsolved Mysteries*. Jenny has great memories watching this with you. Thank you for teaching us both never to give up. Thank you for always being our Wonder Woman.

Love,

Jenny and Jacob

Introduction

Afterword
About the Authors
Bibliography
Also Available
Coming Soon
Excerpts

INTRODUCTION

If you are familiar with the work of the Frightening Floyds, then you know that we are fans of the strange and unusual. In fact, we have an entire paranormal series that carries that name: *Louisville's Strange and Unusual Haunts* and *Indiana's Strange and Usual Haunts* were the first, published with another press and now out of print, but soon to be returning under the Anubis Press banner.

However, it's not only the paranormal that attracts us to that which is strange and unusual. It is also the histories and mysteries behind these paranormal accounts that draw us in. This is also why our interest in strange and unusual events goes beyond the mere paranormal – beyond ghosts and aliens and cryptids, and into unexplained cases of bizarre occurrences, be they disappearances, suspicious murders, areas of the world known for inexplicable and anomalous happenings, or mystifying experiences of unexplainable events. There is so much in the world that is already known, it is imperative that there be those who are attracted to the unknown, for all that is known now was once undiscovered and uncharted, and it takes the curious explorer to uncover new truths. That is what attracts us to that which deviates from the norm, confounds accepted logic, and pushes the limits of belief and imagination.

In the pages ahead, you will read about cases that were unsolved for a long time, and some that still remain as such – stories of people and places that have not quite been concluded or defined, stories that have kept researchers guessing and perplexed for many years. Inspired by a television show that always fascinated both of us – *Unsolved Mysteries* – we dive into some of our favorite mysteries.

Included herein are just a few cases we've studied throughout the years. Jenny's favorite is that of Ogopogo. The idea of a possibly prehistoric creature that has remained hidden in a lake for so long is fascinating. At one time, Jenny had the ambition to be an archeologist, so the notion of previously undiscovered or unclassified species is particularly captivating. Even if the sightings of the creature turn out to be an average lake animal, or even debris, the conceptualization of such a longstanding piece of urban legend is at the root of what we study. So, either way, the story is one of keen interest to her.

For Jacob, it has to be Resurrection Mary. One reason is his lifelong fascination with graveyards. That is something he and Jenny share. He has always been intrigued by the aged stones from times long before he was born, and he's always enjoyed a scary story. Jacob and his friends used to visit allegedly haunted locations long before it was the cool thing to do – long before it was being done to death on television. He was never a ghost hunter until he met Jenny, though he did take pictures in hopes of capturing something spooky; he simply enjoyed the experience of being somewhere alleged to harbor spirits or residual energy. Another reason is the story of Resurrection Mary is so similar to many other hitchhiking ghost stories, or tales of spirits on dark, secluded roads. In fact, there exist two such stories in a book the Frightening Floyds are working on titled *Kentucky's Strange and Unusual Haunts*. Similar stories also exist in many small towns across the country. The folklore, above all, is what is haunting enough.

But those are only a couple of tales that are discussed in this book. The accounts covered in *Strange and Unusual Mysteries* are but a few tales that we have researched. We'd like to thank you, dear reader, for picking up this book and giving it a chance. There's always a strange story to tell, and there's always an unusual answer waiting at the end of its unraveling. The challenge is untying the knots and peeling back the cloak. Once you've done that, you will be the one to know what no one else has yet known. But until you can pull those layers back, the story will remain a mystery.

----- The Frightening Floyds

MOSS BEACH DISTILLERY

Moss Beach Distillery

ocated on the cliffs of Moss Beach in sunny California, the Moss Beach Distillery wasn't always the honest restaurant it is today. Built by Frank Torres in 1927, originally known as Frank's Place, this restaurant was a front for moving whiskey smuggled in by Canadian rum-runners during the Prohibition era. The location overlooked a secluded beach, which made it a perfect spot to conduct such illicit activities. Although the usual destination for the booze was San Francisco, Frank's Place always managed to get its share stored in the basement.

Torres had very powerful social and political connections, as well as some police officers on his payroll, and so his speakeasy was never raided by the Feds. This allowed Frank to continuously conduct his clandestine operation. When

Prohibition ended, Torres stayed in business and ran one of the most successful restaurants along the coast.

Naturally, there were many regulars at the old speakeasy. Politicians as well as silent film actors frequented the joint. Mystery writer Dashiell Hammett (author of *The Maltese Falcon*) even featured Frank's in one of his short stories called "The Girl with the Silver Eyes." As legend has it, there is one regular who has never left, and they call her the Blue Lady.

Moss Beach Distillery from behind

The Blue Lady is a well-known ghost that is believed to have haunted the Moss Beach Distillery since it was known as Frank's Place. According to legend, it was more than 70 years ago that this classy young lady met a man who was a pianist at Frank's Place. This musician was handsome, but dangerous, and though the woman had class, she was very naïve. Some believe she may have been married, which makes it sound as though she wasn't too naive. The woman always wore blue dresses whenever she snuck away to visit her new lover, and that is how people came to know her as the Blue Lady.

One night, as she and the piano man walked along the beach below the restaurant, the man was assaulted by a gang of thugs. He was able to fight them off, but the Blue Lady was mortally wounded in the altercation. None are quite sure who the assailants were, though some think they were gangsters carrying out a hit. Others think maybe the woman's husband discovered the affair and hired someone to kill the couple. The Blue Lady died there on the beach, in the piano player's arms. But her ghost has remained at the restaurant.

Many sightings and strange occurrences have been attributed to the Blue Lady. Women finding their earrings missing only for them to appear somewhere completely different have blamed the ghost. Children spot the lady walking through the restaurant quite often. People's checkbooks have been known to levitate off of tables. Information stored in computers has been changed and removed – don't know how she would have figured that one out since there were no computers in her day, unless her energy somehow affected the data. Empty rooms have inexplicably been locked from inside. Mysterious phone calls come from unknown numbers that cannot be traced (hardly seems paranormal, even if it is eerie). It seems that the Blue Lady, if this is indeed her work, likes to play games, but means no harm as no one has ever been hurt and nothing has ever been damaged by her otherworldly antics.

A parapsychologist by the name of Loyd Auerbach, who also uses the moniker Professor Paranormal, began investigating the distillery in 1991. When *Ghost Hunters* investigated they found several special effects rigged up in the restaurant to give off the impression that the place was haunted. The show made it look as if the owners had set these up to fake customers, and to give weight to the legend of the Blue Lady's presence. The ghost hunters claimed they had no idea the effects were there. However, a contradicting account came from Auerbach.

Apparently, the customers have always known of these effects. They were put in place to add a fun and ghostly atmosphere to the location, leaning on the Blue Lady's legend. Auerbach helped the owners put the devices in place. According to the Professor, he had contacted the producers of *Ghost Hunters* to make them aware of the effects, and the producer told him the investigators already knew they were in the restaurant.

So, is the Moss beach Distillery haunted, or has this mystery always been an elaborate hoax? If the investigators for *Ghost Hunters* were aware of the devices, why would they lie and say they were not? It seems this mystery has been wrapped in another mystery.

The Moss Beach Distillery pier overlooking the ocean

MONA LISA

Mona Lisa

The Mona Lisa by Leonardo Da Vinci is one of the most famous paintings in the world. It is also one of the most valuable, assessed at $100 million in 1962, which equates to a price tag of roughly $650 million today. Painted during the Italian Renaissance, between 1503 and 1517, it has been studied for centuries, and has been at the center of mystery and controversy for some time. The mysterious woman in the foreground of a pastoral backdrop is Lisa, and her identity has been the subject of theory and conjecture since the portrait gained famed. Da Vinci never divulged who this woman was, and took her story with him to the grave.

In 1986, a woman by the name of Lillian Schwartz was navigating a new computer software program and entered in a self-portrait Da Vinci had painted, and when juxtaposed with the Mona Lisa, Schwartz discovered that the two faces bore striking similarities. So alike they were, she determined that Mona Lisa was actually Leonardo Da Vinci himself.

Schwartz then put her theory to a computerized test. Upon entering both portraits for examination, the computer determined that everything matched – the eyes, the nose, and the mouth; when the foreheads were studied, the program found that the super-orbital ridge appearing on both paintings was the type that is most often found in males. Lillian used her program to turn up the corners of the mouth in the self-portrait and found that the result matched Mona Lisa's smile.

Schwartz brought this discovery to the attention of magazine editor Wick Allison in January of 1987. Initially, he dismissed her claim. Once she showed him her scientific evidence, he was convinced. Soon, Schwartz' findings were made public.

Leonardo Da Vinci

While many were convinced of this theory, others remained skeptical. Many said that the alleged self-portrait used in the comparison was a forgery. They also insisted that

Mona Lisa was a wealthy woman from the Renaissance era. But Lillian would not accept these suggestions as fact until she dug a little deeper.

Upon conducting further research, Schwartz discovered an old sketch of an Italian duchess named Isabella by Da Vinci. She believed this was a preliminary drawing of the Mona Lisa, as it matched the painting's under-sketch. However, Schwartz believed that while Da Vinci used Isabella as the foundation for his famous painting, he used his own face to complete it.

Schwartz' work did not go unnoticed. It sparked further research into the mystery, and in 2005 one researcher discovered a margin note that would crack the case. This note was written by a known friend of Da Vinci's, and it contained the identity of the anonymous Mona Lisa. As it turns out, she was not Isabella the Italian duchess, nor was she Da Vinci himself; she was a woman named Lisa del Giocondo.

Da Vinci had taken on the project to paint the wife of Francesco del Giocondo. Born Lisa Gherardini, she was a noblewoman whose roots went back to Tuscany and Florence. She was born in 1479 in Via Maggio, Republic of Florence. She married the silk merchant Francesco when she was only fifteen, becoming the man's third wife. They were not wealthy, but comfortable, and lived a decent life. 'Mona' is Italian for 'My Lady', or 'madonna.'

The Mona Lisa has been copied and parodied numerous times. It is now on display at the Louvre Museum in Paris, France. Through meticulous research, the famous and once enigmatic painting's biggest question has been answered. The Mona Lisa, it seems, is no longer a mystery.

Jenny in front of a Mona Lisa reprint at an Italian restaurant in Louisville

Jacob in front of the same reprint

D.B. COOPER

D.B. Cooper FBI sketch with age progression

November 24th, 1971 is the date of one of the most unusual unsolved FBI cases in history. A nondescript man calling himself Dan Cooper purchased a one-way ticket to Seattle, Washington, using cash, and quickly boarded Flight #305. Cooper was clad in a business suit with a black tie and white shirt, appeared to be somewhere in his 40s – a pretty mundane appearance by all accounts. No doubt, his description matched that of numerous men who board and disembark commercial airlines day in and day out. But Mr. Cooper was far from being the ordinary passenger.

For a man who was about to commit a federal crime, Cooper was pretty nonchalant. As the flight was beginning, he ordered a bourbon and soda and sipped it while patiently waiting for 305 to ascend into the sky. Around 3 pm, Cooper casually slipped a stewardess a note that stated he had an explosive in his briefcase, and requested her to sit with him.

Astonished by this distressing turn of events, she complied. Cooper then opened his case and allowed her a peek at the tangle of wires and red sticks inside, then ordered that she write down what he was about to tell her. Once he had listed his demands – four parachutes and $250,000 in twenty-dollar bills – the stewardess relayed the message to the captain, who then radioed the bizarre hostage situation in to the proper authorities.

After Flight 305 touched down in Seattle, Cooper let the thirty-six passengers on board go free in exchange for the money and chutes. Keeping six members of the crew, he then had the plane take off once again, this time bound for Mexico City.

Around 8 pm, Cooper, no doubt realizing the authorities would be waiting for him at that destination, decided it was time to elude capture. He grabbed the ransom money, took a parachute, and jumped out the back of the Boeing somewhere between Seattle and Reno, Nevada, vanishing into the night. The plane landed safely, no one was hurt, but D.B. Cooper was gone. He left behind only his JC Penney tie, which provided the Feds with some DNA.

The FBI was alerted to the hijacking while 305 was still in the air. They immediately opened a case called NORJACK (Northwest Hijacking), and investigated the incident for a number of years. For half a decade, they interviewed hundreds of suspects across the nation, and eliminated all but around two dozen. They searched the aircraft top to bottom, but were unable to uncover anything of use.

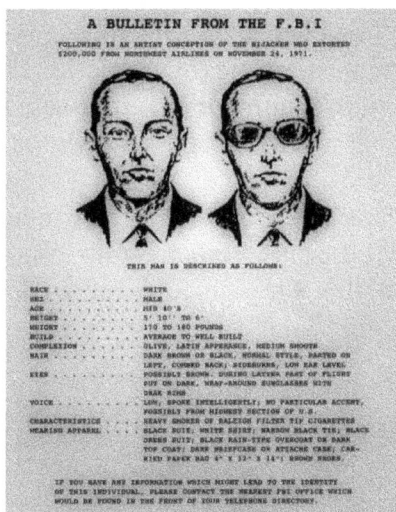

FBI bulletin for D.B. Cooper

One of the FBI's prime suspects, Richard Floyd McCoy, was arrested for a similar hijacking and parachute escape not long after Cooper's. While the lead seemed promising at first, McCoy had to eventually be released because he did not match the description given by two flight attendants. That was the hottest lead they've had to date.

To this day, Cooper's identity remains a mystery. It is quite possible that he did not survive the landing. His parachute was not one that could be steered, and he was not properly dressed for such a landing. He vacated the plane over a wooded area, which would have been dangerous even for a professional skydiver – which all evidence suggests he was not.

In 1980, a young boy found a package of deteriorated twenty-dollar bills that equaled about $5800 somewhere in the vicinity of where Cooper would have landed, with serial numbers matching those that were on the ransom money. This finding lends support to the idea that the hijacker died after his escape.

If he didn't however, then this anonymous man pulled off one of the greatest crimes in aviation history, in broad daylight, in front of a number of witnesses. If his daring jump paid off, then it seems D.B. Cooper, whoever he is, is possibly the most elusive criminal the FBI has ever encountered. This leads a person to wonder if he pulled off any other great heists. Perhaps this question will remain unanswered as this strange and unusual mystery remains unsolved.

Richard Floyd McCoy, the FBI's best lead so far

BERMUDA TRIANGLE

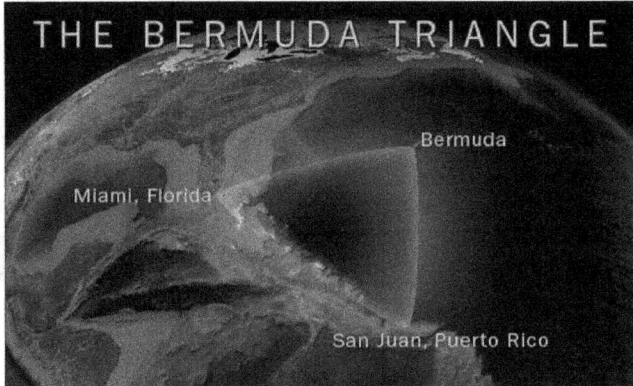

The location of the Bermuda Triangle

One of the world's eeriest and most enigmatic locations is the mythical Bermuda Triangle, which is bordered by Miami, Bermuda, and Puerto Rico. Also called the Devil's Triangle, this section of the Atlantic Ocean has become legendary for missing ships, vanishing airplanes, and unexplainable mechanical malfunctions. But it's not just the simple disappearances and technological breakdowns that have people baffled. Some of the unusual events surrounding these incidents have added to the intrigue.

On a more personal note, before we get into the strange phenomena surrounding this location, we'd just like to mention that Jenny's mother once swam in the Bermuda Triangle near Miami. Part of the reason she has chosen to dedicate this book to her mother is for her adventuresome spirit, but also because it was her who helped spark Jenny's interest in the strange and unusual. But, something else to consider – Jenny's mother entered the Triangle with no vessel and never went missing.

There have been other accounts of ships vanishing in good weather, without any distress signals or other attempted contact with the mainland. Naturally, this fills people with fear and suspicion regarding the Triangle, but there is no actual evidence that supports the theory that more ships and planes vanish in that area of the Atlantic than any other regularly travelled water way. Vessels navigate the Bermuda Triangle often without incident.

The Bermuda Triangle covers about 500,000 square miles off the southeastern shore of Florida. Stories of peculiar experiences date back as far as the voyage of Christopher Columbus to the New World. He left behind a report that described a great ball of flame crashing into the ocean, and a light appearing in the sky a few weeks later. This very well could have been a meteor landing in the waters. Although it is extremely unlikely, perhaps this impact caused a disruption in the magnetic field. He also reported strange compass readings in the area, but at that time, a small portion of the Triangle was one of the only places on the planet where true north aligned with the magnetic north.

The first incident to really draw attention to the Bermuda Triangle occurred in March of 1918 when a Navy cargo ship more than 500 feet long, carrying 10,000 tons of manganese ore, and with a crew of more than 300 men, went down in the Triangle without a distress call. This ship was known as the USS *Cyclops* and it sank into the oceanic depths somewhere between Barbados and the Chesapeake Bay. None of the wreckage was ever recovered, making the matter much more mysterious. In 1941, two of the *Cyclops'* sister ships disappeared mysteriously along the same route.

According to legend, similar disappearances began to occur frequently in the Triangle. Another notable case happened in 1945 when five Navy bombers were flying over the area and began to have compass malfunctions. This led to the planes getting lost. Pilots began sending back peculiar and distressing messages describing the unusual appearance of everything around them. They flew aimlessly until they ran out of fuel and went down. Later that day, the Navy sent in a rescue plane, but it too, along with the thirteen men on board, vanished. The Navy scoured that area of the Atlantic for a week and found no evidence that would reveal what might have happened. The official report was that it was like the planes simply went to Mars.

That area of the ocean didn't get its official nickname of the Bermuda Triangle until author Vincent Gaddis said it in a 1964 magazine article. By this time, there had been more incidents of unexplained disappearances. Among them were three passenger planes that crashed after sending their 'all's well' messages.

Since then, many paranormal theories have been offered to explain the bizarre events that happen in the Bermuda Triangle. It's been said that the Lost City of Atlantis has something to do with them, others say extraterrestrials are involved. Sea monster attacks have even been suggested. People have theorized that a reverse gravity field exists in the Triangle. There are even those who believe time warping is to blame. Those who are skeptical about such possibilities believe the disappearances can be attributed to issues with the magnetic fields in the Triangle, massive eruptions of methane gas exploding from the ocean floor, and waterspouts.

The truth is probably that there is no single explanation to encompass each incident. As with the rest of the world's oceans, ships can go down for a variety of reasons. The same conclusion can be reached for the disappearances of planes. Experts believe there is nothing unusual about the events that have transpired in the alleged Bermuda Triangle. Despite that, many cases remain a mystery.

FACE ON MARS

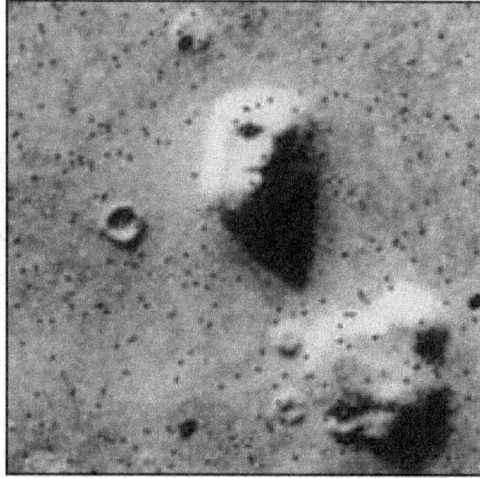

The original "Face on Mars" photograph

In 1976, NASA's *Viking 1* spacecraft circled Mars, taking photographs of the planet's surface in search of a potential landing site for *Viking 2*. One of the photographs returned a fascinating image. Rising from the ground of an area known as Cydonia, was a two-mile-wide mound that resembled a human face. Though the image probably caused a stir back at the Jet Propulsion Lab, NASA scientists that were on hand quickly debunked it as nothing more than a common Martian mesa – a mesa that just happened to resemble the head of an Egyptian pharaoh.

Despite having quickly discovered what the image truly was, NASA decided to release the photo to the public in order to generate interest in the mission. They didn't present it falsely, and were quite open about what the formation actually was, but it did gain Mars some attention, and perhaps it wasn't the kind of attention folks at NASA were expecting.

The "Face on Mars" image has become a cultural phenomenon. It has been seen hanging around on tabloid covers in the checkout lines at grocery stores for several decades. It's been shown in films, on television, and included in books and magazines. The Face has sparked conspiracy theories that the picture is evidence of alien life on Mars, and that NASA seeks to cover it up. Though no NASA scientists seemed to think this mesa was any sort of evidence of alien life, they did make photographing Cydonia a top priority when the Mars Global Surveyor arrived at the planet eighteen years later.

On April 5th, 1998, MGS was able to take a photograph that was ten times sharper than the *Viking 1* snapshot. The photo was then uploaded online not long after it was taken. When those eager to see the truth signed on to view it, they were no doubt disappointed to discover that the mesa was nothing more than a natural landform, and not an alien monument at all.

But this did not stop the hardcore believers. It was soon pointed out that when the new picture was taken, it was wintertime in Cydonia, and the camera had to take the shot through wispy winter clouds hovering in the atmosphere. Some insisted that the alien markings were distorted by the cloudy haze.

Mars controllers were willing to take another shot, despite the difficulty involved. It seems that the MGS does not pass over the Face all that often. But they assured the public they would be ready when the next time came around.

That day came on April 8th, 2001, on what would be a clear summer day in the Cydonia region. Controllers made sure to rotate the camera and position it just right over the face and were able to take a perfect picture with the camera's maximum resolution. It was clear. The Face is inarguably a Martian mesa, not uncommon from a butte or mesa in the

American west, and contains no superficial evidence of alien life on the Red Planet. In fact, further examination with other technologies has returned evidence that the Face mound is ultimately no different than the many other mounds scattered across the face of the world.

So, as exciting as it would be to be able to point to the mound as evidence of alien life, especially so near to our own planet, those who were once hopeful will have to look elsewhere. The case of the Face on Mars is no longer a mystery.

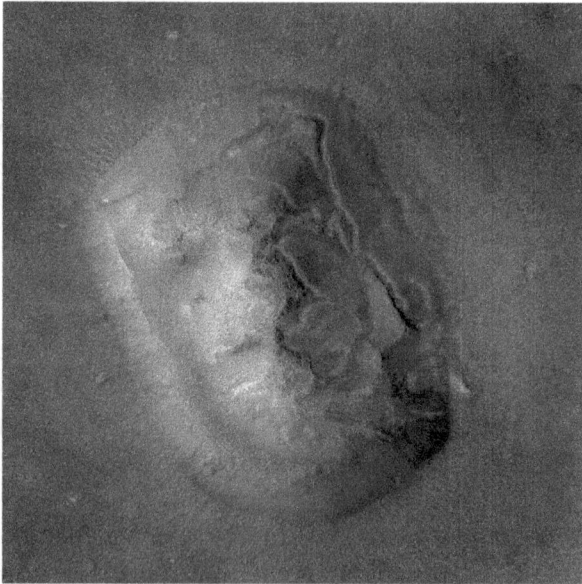

A clearer photo of the "Face on Mars"

GULF BREEZE UFO

In November of 1987, the *Gulf Breeze Sentinel* published an article about an alleged UFO sighting, complete with pictures from a man named Ed Walters. Walters claimed the pictures showed a large UFO traveling down the road near his home in Gulf Breeze, Florida. For the next year, people in the area began watching the sky, hoping to spot an alien craft. Many UFOlogists believed in the authenticity of the photographs, but there were others who were skeptical.

Perhaps the most vocal skeptic at the time was a reporter for the *Pensacola News Journal* named Craig Myers. He was hypercritical of the *Sentinel*'s piece about the claim, calling it sensationalist and uncritical. He decided to investigate the case on his own and briefly moved into the house Walters lived in at the time of the alleged sighting – Walters having since moved from the house. Myers claimed to have found a Styrofoam model of the exact UFO appearing in the photographs, and was able to recreate the pictures. This, he claimed, debunked Walters' case.

Walters, on the other hand, had another explanation. Still sticking to his guns, he replied that the pictures were genuine and that Myers simply made the replica and lied about finding it in the attic. Walters claimed no such replica ever existed when he occupied the home. But many still believe the incident was staged – even the writers of the classic television series *The X-Files* believed it was a hoax and voiced this through the character, Fox Mulder. Others claimed to have known personally that the sighting was a hoax.

Myers believed that the Gulf Breeze UFO incident was a hoax so adamantly that he wrote a book about it, and sometimes gives lectures on it. Though Myers does not believe the incident was remotely authentic, he does not speak maliciously of Walters. He has stated that many people knew Walters to be a prankster anyway, and even admits that the incident probably began as an innocent prank that snowballed, also insisting that Walters is probably a highly intelligent individual.

Ed and his wife, Frances, also wrote a book about the incident, as did UFO researcher, Bruce Maccabee, who believes Walters' claim. He echoed the same explanation that the model was in fact staged, as opposed to the actual incident. Much like Myers, he too has written technical papers and articles about it. But with Maccabee being a physicist as well, he brings a little more credibility to the table.

In his defense of Walters' claim he mentioned that even if you took his incident out of the equation, you still have a large number of other reported sightings in the Gulf Breeze area. With hundreds of residents watching the skies, there were well over a dozen very detailed and similar reports, even though none were as vivid as that of Ed Walters. Even local politicians have made claims about seeing odd objects in the sky. So unless a large number of the populace is in on the prank, including city officials, you cannot entirely dismiss Walters' photographs.

George Williams, state director of the Florida Mutual UFO Network in Tallahassee doesn't really have a strong opinion on whether or not Walters faked the photographs. He seems to think it would be a strange and unlikely act that Walters would create the model and then bury it beneath the insulation in his attic. MUFON investigated the claim, and went back and forth on the matter many times, but never did reach a conclusion regarding Walters' pictures. Regardless,

Williams says that Gulf Breeze is a real UFO hotspot and they continue to get reports from there.

Even though it seems Gulf Breeze is an active location for extraterrestrial travelers, people still have a hard time believing Ed Walters. Whether or not his photographs were authentic still remains a mystery.

A sketch of the alleged Gulf Breeze UFO

OGOPOGO

Ogopogo, also known as Oggy, N'ha-a-itk, and Naitaka, is a mythological lake monster from Canadian folklore said to live beneath the waters of Okanagan Lake in British Columbia. Historians believe that his origin derives from legends told by the First Nations. It is said that the Secwepemc and Syilx tribes regarded Naitaka as an evil supernatural entity that demanded sacrifices in exchange for safe passage across the lake. This led to the Nations offering small animals to the waters for hundreds of years.

Naitaka, as legend has it, would use its tail to create storms in the water, and send any trespassers to their deaths. A man by the name of Sir John Lambton was said to have killed a wyrm from the lake, and in doing so visited a witch's curse upon all of his descendants. Author Susan Allison was the first non-Native to see Ogopogo, reporting to have spotted him in the lake in 1872.

A man by the name of Art Folden spotted the creature moving around the lake as he drove down Highway 97 in 1968. He stopped his vehicle to film the monster. The video, he claimed, showed a large wake in the water which was being made by Ogopogo, who was about 300 yards away. The footage underwent a computer analysis and it was determined that there was definitely a three-dimensional object in the water beneath that wake. Whether or not it was Ogopogo is an entirely different story.

In 2005, two avid skeptics, Benjamin Radford and Joe Nickell, and John Kirk of the National Geographic television program, *Is It Real?*, reviewed the video and investigated the claim. Using surveyor boats to measure the distance between Folden and the wake, they concluded that the distance had initially been overestimated, thus causing the size and speed of the wake to appear much larger and faster than they actually were. They theorized that what Folden had filmed was likely a water fowl or otter. How truly conclusive their findings are is hard to say.

In 1980, as many as fifty tourists watched what they believed to be Ogopogo swimming in the lake for nearly forty-five minutes. One man managed to capture ten seconds of footage, but skeptics said it was two otters he had filmed. John Kirk, however, said he saw a creature that was anywhere between ten to twelve meters long with five sleek bumps on its back and a lashing tail moving at a pace of about twenty-five miles per hour.

Over the years, there have been many other videos and alleged sightings of Ogopogo, most very easy to debunk. The usual answers are otters, water fowl, debris, or logs. However, just because the waters may be full of such things, it does not debunk the possibility that the peculiar sightings could be the legendary Ogopogo. Is he out there? To this day, we still don't know, and so his existence remains a mystery.

THE YETI

Also known as the Abominable Snowman, the Yeti is one of the most famous cryptids in the entire world. Known for lurking about in the Himalayan mountains, the first bit of evidence of the Yeti dates back to 1951, and since then many Western explorers have traveled to the Himalayas in search of the elusive creature, only to find some very astonishing evidence and hear some interesting stories of an ape-like humanoid living in the region.

In 1951, a world-renowned mountaineer by the name of Eric Shipton discovered a very curious set of footprints in the freezing snow atop the mountains. The tracks showed individual toes on a foot that was thirteen inches long and eight inches wide.

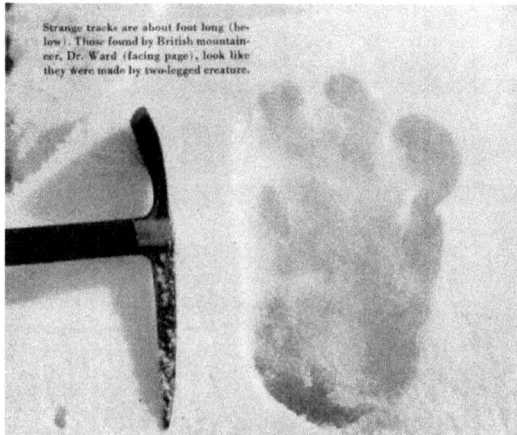

Strange tracks are about foot long (below). Those found by British mountaineer, Dr. Ward (facing page), look like they were made by two-legged creature.

Possible Yeti footprint in the snow

In 1957, Texas oilman Tom Slick and explorer Peter Byrne embarked upon a trip to the Arun Valley in northeastern Nepal to seek out the mythical monster. Once they found the Sherpas – the region's indigenous people – they spoke about the Yeti. The Sherpas referred to the creature as a hairy man that lived away from them. When they were shown a set of pictures containing a chimpanzee, gorilla, and primitive man, they would point to the primitive man as being like the Yeti. But unlike its counterpart, Bigfoot, the Yeti is not a towering monster. The Sherpas described him as being only about 5'8'' and hairy, walking upright, and with a hairless face. In another part of the valley, they found another set of footprints, similar to Shipton's discovery, only smaller.

In February of the following year, Byrne returned to the area and met a Buddhist monk who showed him a preserved hand believed to have belonged to a Yeti. It was about the size of a human hand and it had been severed at the wrist. The monk would not permit the hand to leave the temple, so Byrne took photographs of it. When he showed the photographs to scientists, they proclaimed they had never seen any hands like it.

Byrne returned the next year with a plan to cut a finger off the hand and replace it with a fake. After giving the monk a bottle of Scotch, Byrne proceeded with his plan. He said it took him quite a while to wire the hand back together, but he was able to claim the finger for which he had come.

Byrne brought the finger back to London and gave it to a Dr. George Agogino. The doctor presented the specimen to twenty more experts, and the consensus was divided among them as to whether or not the finger belonged to a human or a primate of either known or unknown origins. Dr. Agogino then took a tissue sample from the finger and placed it in an envelope on his desk, where it sat for more than thirty years.

The crew at *Unsolved Mysteries* had the finger analyzed by scientists at the University of California. The test results were inconclusive, but leaned heavily in favor of the finger belonging to a human hand. However, the Professor of Nuclear Medicine who examined the finger, Dr. Jerry Lowenstein, maintained that no matter what creature the finger came from, it neither proves nor disproves the existence of the Yeti.

Reports of the creature continued. A photographer named Kurt Fritler encountered a Yeti at his campsite 16,500 feet into the Himalayas. He described a loud piercing howl echoing in the night before the creature came and circled his campsite. A man named Reinhold Messner claimed to have seen the creature from about thirty feet away and described it has being dark brown with very long hairs, short legs, and very powerful.

Stories of the Yeti have continued to circulate throughout the decades. Though the debate about the creature's existence remains unresolved, a DNA test was conducted on the bone fragment once again in 2011. Results determined the finger did indeed come from a human hand. Dr. Lowenstein's assertion that the finger's origin having no real connection to whether or not the mysterious Yeti actually exists stands true, and many believe the creature is indeed very real. But until the day a Yeti is discovered, this claim will remain a mystery.

Possible Yeti tracks with a possible Yeti in the distance

NOAH'S ARK

Formation believed by some to be the remains of Noah's Ark

The Biblical tale of Noah's Ark is about one man rescuing the human race from a great deluge delivered by God. According to the story, God spoke to Noah and told him of the flood many years in advance. He ordered Noah to build a great ark that could carry two of each animal species and his family. He did so, and when the flood came, the ark saved all on board.

As with many stories in the Bible, there are many people who challenge the tale of Noah, finding it to be very unlikely that such a construct could have been created in that time, not to mention there is no geological evidence of such a massive flood in the world's history. However, there are those who believe that the ark can be found in the snow-capped dormant volcano Mount Ararat in the extreme eastern portion of Turkey, where the Bible states it would have stopped sailing. This location is very dangerous and difficult to reach. However, of the numerous expeditions into the nearly inaccessible mountains, two groups believe they may have found the remains of the ark in separate locations some seventeen miles apart.

In 1906, when Turkish businessman George Hagobian was a young boy, he believed he saw the ark protruding from a large glacier that had partially melted on the mountain's northeast side when he ventured there with his uncle. He gave a very detailed description of the measurements, angles, and even of the surface where he was able to briefly explore, to archeological illustrator Elfred Lee. Upon returning to the location in his later years, he found that the ice and snow had reclaimed the section that had been uncovered when he was a child.

In 1986, Lee met a US Army official named Ed Davis, who was stationed in Iran. Davis claimed to have seen the ark several times in the same location as Hagobian during flights over the mountain. The description he gave was almost identical to that of Hagobian's, with only one differing trait. According to Davis, the ark had broken in two after years of heavy ice and snow weighing it down. He also claimed that he was able to see the sunlight going all the way to the bottom deck of the massive vessel, and was able to see the many cages left inside.

Mt. Ararat

Though Davis and Hagobian's accounts could only offer a rough estimation as to the location of the giant glacier allegedly holding Noah's Ark, their stories caught the attention of archeologist Don Shockey. Shockey headed an expedition into Mount Ararat in April of 1989 after being permitted to study classified aerial photos of the mountain. He and his team spent three days climbing the south side of the mountain, but were denied access to the north side by the Turkish government.

One of his guides, a Turkish man named Ahmet, continued to climb the mountain alone. When he made it to nearly 16,000 feet, he saw something buried halfway in the snow and took a photograph of it. The picture revealed a rectangular object with a peaked roof about 300 yards away. Ahmet said he thought the picture showed only a chicken coup, but Shockey suspected it could have been a piece of Noah's Ark.

Shockey then took the picture to an anthropologist by the name of Dr. Jim Ebert. Ebert studied the photograph and determined that whatever the subject was, it was definitely man-made. This prompted Shockey to return to the mountain in 1990. Unfortunately, upon arrival, he discovered that the area in the picture had been once again covered in snow, and whatever had been sticking out was now engulfed by the ice. That was the end of Shockey's search, but he was convinced they had glimpsed Noah's Ark.

David Fasold, an ark researcher and former merchant marine officer and marine salvage expert, disputes Shockey's claim. Fasold believes that the resting place of Noah's Ark lies seventeen miles to the south of Mt. Ararat. During his own investigation in the late 1980s, Fasold and his team discovered many iron fittings and pins that, after meticulous examination, formed a pattern very much like that of the ark. Measurements of the frame put the object at 515 feet in length and 85 in width, which is believed to be the measurements from the Bible. Other experts and researchers contest that what Fasold found was either a geological formation or an ancient Mongol fort. The Turkish government, however, believes the ark lies there beneath the earth, and has officially named the site the burial place of Noah's Ark.

The debate continues today. No doubt others will seek to uncover the truth about what remains frozen in the large glacier upon Mount Ararat, or what lies buried seventeen miles to the south. Until they do and can determine what exactly is beneath the ice, whether or not Noah's Ark exists will remain a mystery.

Another view of the formation

RESURRECTION CEMETERY

The gates of Resurrection Cemetery

L ocated in Justice, IL, on the southwest side of Chicago, Resurrection Cemetery is one of the most famous haunted cemeteries in the U.S. Unexplainable activity has been reported about the location since early 1979.

There have been many accounts of a ghostly hitchhiker picked up near the cemetery, who disappears shortly after getting into the vehicle. A local folklorist and historian, Richard Crowe, believes in the hitchhiking apparition. He says that most of the people he has spoken to about it are levelheaded individuals who have never made any other paranormal claims in their lives.

The first case reported was in 1939. Taxi driver Jerry Palus picked up a blonde woman at the gates of the cemetery. Immediately taken by her beauty, he asked her out on a date to a local dance hall. She accepted and during the date, he learned her name was Mary and she came from the south side of town. While they danced, Palus noticed Mary was very cold. Once the date was over, the cabbie offered her a ride home. She asked him to drop her off at the gates of another cemetery located on Archer Road. He obliged and after she vacated the vehicle, she vanished right in front of him.

Palus was baffled by what he had just witnessed. So, he drove to the house where she had previously told him she lived. Upon arrival, he was met by her mother, who was quite confused as to why this strange man was at her door in the middle of the night. He recounted to her his encounter with Mary and her mother told him something that chilled him. She explained to Palus that Mary had died five years ago.

Another well known encounter is that of the patrolmen who kept an eye on the cemetery at night. One night they spotted a figure inside the gates. Thinking someone had accidentally been locked inside, they found the caretaker and told him about it. Once they all got back to the gates, the figure was gone. But whoever it was had not vanished without a trace. They had left behind some bent bars with small handprints upon them.

Clare Rudnicki claimed that she and her husband Mark saw Mary walking past the graveyard in 1980 as they drove by. They quickly turned around and went back, but when they returned to the cemetery, she had disappeared. Clare stated that she had heard the tales of Resurrection Cemetery before, but didn't believe them. However, what she witnessed that night might have changed her mind. She said that as they passed the woman, Rudnicki could see that she was glowing so bright she looked illuminated. When they noticed she had vanished, Rudnicki realized that she may have just seen Resurrection Mary.

A woman named Janet Kalal claimed that she and a friend bore witness to the ghost of Mary in October of 1989. As they passed Resurrection Cemetery, a pale young woman dressed in white with her hair flowing out behind her stepped in front of the car. Janet could not stop in time to miss her and they ran right into the woman. Though there was no forceful impact and no bump beneath the car, both women knew they had hit her. When they got out to look, the young woman was nowhere to be found.

One group of friends had a bit more frightening encounter with Mary. As they drove by the cemetery late one night, they saw a woman beneath the light on the gate, and where her face was supposed to be, they saw nothing but darkness. Unlike the previous stories, these witnesses did not decide to turn around and say hello to the resident specter.

Accounts of encounters with Resurrection Mary have been reported countless times through the years. She has been spotted in taxi cabs, dance halls, and walking the grounds in and around Resurrection Cemetery, looking for someone to take her home. Whether or not they are true reports, accurate, or whether or not one believes in the spirit, Mary was a real person.

In 1934, a young lady named Mary Bregovy died in an automobile accident a month before her twenty-first birthday. She was interred at Resurrection Cemetery wearing her favorite white gown. When the graveyard underwent a restructuring, Mary's remains were relocated, and those who believe in her ghost theorize that she now wanders the area in search of her original resting place. However, if she is often asking people for a ride home, she might not realize she is dead and may be simply trying to go home.

Whether or not Mary is angry at the moving of her remains, or wants a ride home, or exists in spirit at Resurrection Cemetery at all remains a mystery.

THE ICEMAN

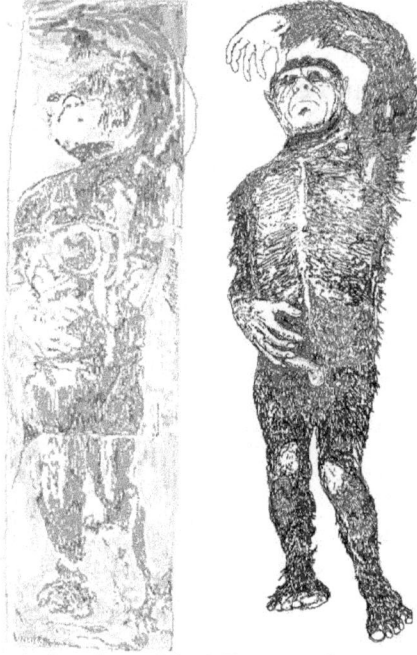

A drawing of the Minnesota Iceman

The Minnesota Iceman is a humanoid cryptid with ape-like features found frozen in a block of ice. The creature stands about six feet tall, is covered in hair, and appears to have a traumatic injury on the left side of his face. In 1967 and 1968, the "Ice Man" was displayed at carnivals and state fairs all throughout the Midwest. Of the thousands that viewed him, none could quite figure out what he was.

There are, however, many people who have seen the Iceman and believe he is a deceased primitive man. Experts that have viewed him also profess that they can tell he is not man-made or mechanical, and some believe him to be a dead animal of some kind. There are skeptics that present compelling arguments that the creature is actually a rubber gaff, noting that during its last transport, a lot of the ice melted and nothing much changed about the creature's corpse. Also, there was no concern on the part of the new owner for the defrosting, and no efforts were even made to keep it frozen, which skeptics feel is indicative of the creature's artificial nature.

Dr. Terry Cullen, a veterinarian and zoological researcher, saw the Iceman when he was seventeen and noted that there was a distinct aroma coming from him, and he also concluded that it is made of flesh. He returned many times in his life to conduct further examinations of the creature, even sneaking in a magnifying glass on one occasion. He could discern a few details about the Iceman. One was that he appeared to have a death grimace on his face. Another was that his lips were pulled back, revealing four incisors, which Cullen noted were square, much like an orangutan's.

So intrigued was Cullen by the Iceman that he took great effort in attempting to get scientists to study the specimen to determine whether it was fake or an unknown primitive species. Eventually, he was able to persuade an anthropologist from the University of Minnesota to study the Iceman. The anthropologist examined the creature for about fifteen minutes before leaving. The anthropologist confessed to being amazed by the Iceman, but would say little else.

All of this began when the creature fell into the possession of a man named Frank Hansen in 1967. Hansen showed the creature to many scientists and other people at fairs. The Iceman became national news in 1969, attracting the attention of the FBI, who wanted to see the creature in case it was a murder victim. Hansen agreed to show a visiting agent the Iceman, and the agent said he would return the following day with a pathologist to have it thoroughly examined. That night, Hansen left town with the frozen corpse. He then began showing up at fairs with a replica, and no one had seen the real body for decades. He also later claimed that the Iceman was nothing more than a rubber hoax.

When asked, Hansen would not talk about the Iceman. However, before he had decided to go silent on the matter, he had told the story of how he came to possess him. He stated that as he was travelling the fair circuit displaying an old mechanical contraption that he proclaimed was the first gas-powered tractor, he was approached by a very discreet individual who presented him with his business card and told him that he possessed an exhibit that he felt Hansen would be interested in. Hansen later contacted the stranger and met him at a refrigerated warehouse at an undisclosed location. The stranger unveiled the Iceman, who was then stored in a box. He told Hansen that he had found the creature in Minnesota, but Hansen has changed his story since, saying that the man told him the body was found somewhere in Siberia. Hansen agreed to take the creature on the road and bill him as an educational exhibit.

At the request of Terry Cullen, crypto-zoologists Ivan T. Sanderson and Dr. Bernard Heuvelmans visited Hansen's barn in December of 1968 and examined the Iceman. They decided that it was a prehistoric relative of man that somehow survived into the 20th century. They also stated that he had severe head injuries on the left side of his face.

In 2013, it was alleged that the Iceman had been found and was purchased by the owner of the Museum of the Weird through eBay. The buyer claims that he purchased the Iceman from an individual who bought him from Hansen's family after Hansen passed away in 2003. While many believe the Iceman is real and could be a missing link between Neanderthals and modern man, others believe the creature is a hoax.

Until they remove the creature from the ice and conduct a thorough examination, it seems the authenticity of the Minnesota Iceman will remain a mystery.

MEXICO CITY UFO

During the solar eclipse that took place on July 11th, 1991, residents of Mexico City gazed into the darkened sky that afternoon and saw something many thought was more astonishing than the last total eclipse of the century. What they saw was a round, metallic object with blinking lights floating through the sky. One witness said there was even an energy trail expelled from the back of the craft.

Journalist Jaime Maussan and reporter Guillermo Arraign were recording the eclipse for Mexico's version of *60 Minutes* when they saw the UFO. They managed to get footage of it crossing the sky. Once the footage aired, thousands of calls came in from others who claimed to have seen the craft. It seemed many other individuals were filming, as several videos were sent to the station.

A group of friends were setting up a camera on a rooftop in preparation to record the eclipse when someone noticed the object in the sky. At first, they all could just see a small dot in the air, but as it progressed, they could see that the object was shiny.

Luis Lara filmed an identical object about sixty miles away. He spotted a shadow beneath it, which proved it was not a star.

Nearly eighty miles away in Puebla, the Breton family also videotaped the UFO. This video showed some details that weren't present in the others. It showed the craft as a pulsating disc with some sort of wavy disturbance trailing along behind it. Despite the extra details, and being about 100 miles apart, this video was very similar to many others.

Two months later, Vicente Sanchez was filming some planes during a military show in Mexico City when he noticed a small shiny dot in the distance. The dot was round, bright, and roughly ten meters in diameter. He suspected the shininess was due to sunlight reflecting off the craft's silver surface.

The same air show yielded similar UFO sightings the following year in 1993. After the alien excitement of the last two years, many were expecting to see the UFO. They got their wish when a squadron of helicopters flew over the city. The shiny dot returned to the sky, and was moving against the wind. It also appeared to be very near to the helicopters.

Since the 1991 sightings, thousands of people have reported seeing this shiny dot. The bulk of the reports come out of Mexico City, the most heavily populated city in the country. The military have not issued a response to these incidents, and no one has been able to explain these sightings. Some claim that the object in question was actually the planet Venus, though that explanation is often disputed. Whether the object was a planet, a plane, or an alien craft remains a mystery.

THE BLINKING CRUCIFIX

In the small town of Ambridge, Pennsylvania, about twenty miles to the north of Pittsburgh, many parishioners of the Holy Trinity Church believed they witnessed a miracle during Good Friday in 1989.

Though the town has been dying for some time due to many of its steel mills closing, the people refuse to leave. With their faith unwavering, they gather at the Holy Trinity Church every Sunday. The church has had a large crucifix suspended inside the service area since 1931. In 1989, an artist named Domenic Leo spent many hours working diligently to restore the crucifix's original image, and said that he paid special attention to the eyes.

On March 24th, during a three hour mass for Good Friday, with more than 300 attendees, an altar boy named Jim Cvitkovic looked up at the crucifix while praying during the Holy Communion and believed its eyes, that had always been open, were now closed. This incident shocked him, but also brought him joy.

Jim asked his brother Tom to confirm this event. Tom thought the eyes looked to be closed as well, but was unsure if this was a trick of the light or not. So, he went around to the other side of the crucifix to get a better look and discovered that it did indeed appear as if Jesus' eyes were closed.

Once the mass had concluded, the brothers, who were now weeping, went to their uncle, Reverend Vincent Cvitkovic, and told him of their finding. The reverend and another priest looked at the crucifix and also noticed that its eyes were closed. Vincent then called for the artist to take a look, and Leo was surprised to see that the eyes looked to be closed. More than that, Leo believed he saw tears coming from the eyes as they moved around inside the statue's head. This caused Leo to begin weeping as well.

A ladder was brought in so people could get a closer look, as it was difficult to discern the details of the statue's face since the crucifix hung twenty-two feet above the floor. Leo was first to ascend the ladder and take a look. Upon closer inspection, he determined that the left eye had closed completely and the right eye was only slightly open.

As whispers of a miracle began to mutter through the crowd, state trooper Chris Marion, who was also a parishioner, decided to climb the ladder and have a look to ensure that no one had created this illusion. Though skeptical as he peered into the statue's face, he became convinced that no one had tampered with it. Also, knowing his fellow parishioners well, he believed wholeheartedly that no one present would have perpetrated such a hoax.

Sue Tolfa was very familiar with the crucifix, and had often seen it when it used to hang in an alcove with lighted candles beneath it. She knew that the eyes were open every day, until that day. She too was convinced of the miracle, for she could plainly see that the eyes were now shut.

Later that night, another parishioner claimed to have received a divine message as he stood in the church gazing up at the miraculous crucifix. He wrote the message down and read it to the rest of the church. It spoke of showing the parishioners a sign, for Jesus was appreciative of their devotion to Him. In the note, it was said that in the months to come, thousands would come to see what He had done, and He told the people of Ambridge to accept the visitors.

As predicted, thousands did come to see the crucifix. Many believe it was a hoax or hallucination, but there are many more who are convinced that the statue of Jesus upon the cross did in fact close its eyes.

Catholic scholar Suzanne Reinee is skeptical of the supposed miracle. She thinks the parishioners, in their passionate faith, saw something they wanted to see as opposed to something that was truly there. The Catholic Church echoes this skepticism and they have stated they will not officially document this incident as a true miracle until several necessary steps have been taken to investigate and confirm the alleged event. They prefer that people return to the church for the right reasons and not for some perceived miracle that did not actually occur.

Once the miracle was supposedly discounted, the pastor resigned. He passed away in August of 2004. Domenic Leo died in 2017. Though there were still several witnesses who claimed this miracle did in fact happen, all entities with the authority to officially declare the incident a miracle have determined no miracle occurred. Now that the two men closest to the incident are gone, this case is almost certain to remain a mystery.

E.L.F. (EXTREMELY LOW FREQUENCY)

Extremely Low Frequency, also called the Taos Hum for Taos, New Mexico, where reports of the hum began in 1970, is an unexplained hum heard by people at a very low frequency around the world. This unidentified "hum" cannot be heard by everyone, but is heard by thousands of people.

Among them is Hal Runniano of Michigan. Hal claims to have first heard the hum after moving to a small lake side town outside of Detroit. Initially, he thought it was the sound of a diesel engine idling nearby. But after a while, when it did not change or stop, it started to become a serious distraction to his daily life. Hal checked many places where he believed the hum could have been emanating from, such as the local airport and university ventilation systems, but he could never pin down the sound. It was suggested to Hal that he could be hearing something coming from an electromagnetic field. He was then told to go to a nearby copper mine and see if he could still hear the hum below ground. When he went into the mine, not only could he still hear the hum, it actually became louder and clearer.

A Taos radio broadcast engineer named Sarah Allen is another person who hears the Taos Hum. She began to hear the sound after being sent to repair a broken radio transmitter in 1992. She was able to play a digital recording of what the hum sounds like to her for a woman named Winona Whitthead who lives in neighboring Santa Fe. Winona has been hearing the hum since 1990 and she agreed that the sound on the recording sounds very much like what she hears as well. The hum has affected Winona so badly that she had to quit her job at the National Parks Services and get on disability.

The hum is so disruptive to many people that a support group has formed. Many believe the hum comes from an extremely low frequency created by the Navy to communicate with submarine vessels on the ocean floor, since standard radio waves cannot penetrate the water. E.L.F. has been in use since the 1980s and has been heard all around the world.

Taos has been investigated by scientists with extensive sound studying devices. They have found nothing out of the ordinary to cause the hum. Doctors examined Hal to see if the hum could be caused by some sort of hearing issue. Though Hal was experiencing hearing loss, the doctors found no anomalies that could be causing the hum.

Though the Taos Hum has stumped many doctors and scientists, some have come up with a theoretical explanation in recent years. It is thought that the hum is caused by sea waves colliding with the ocean. Studies show that North America's Pacific Coast is where the hum is heard the most. What happens is when two waves of similar frequencies moving in opposite directions meet, it sends a frequency speeding to the ocean floor. When that frequency hits the rocks, it causes a vibration that releases this low humming sound. The reason the hum is constant for those who hear it is because this wave interaction happens non-stop at different locations around the world.

While this theory sounds pretty wild, it has been scientifically studied using seismographs, which can detect this low frequency easily enough. A variety of scientific data was captured with a device called the USArray EarthScope. Scientists were able to determine that the coast of Europe produces a very distinct hum as well. Most data concludes that E.L.F. happens mostly in coastal towns, which makes

Taos being its original location rather contradictory, considering it is nowhere near a coast of any kind.

There have also been studies that suggest that two-thirds of the people who experience the hum are acutely focused on the many background noises surrounding them in their daily lives. Others believe the hum is created by animal noises blending together. Naturally, mechanical devices, such as diesel engines and other machinery, have been blamed. Some medical experts opined that tinnitus could be to blame, but variables such as the hum being louder outdoors than indoors, and changing depending on the environment, challenge this theory. Spontaneous otoacoustic emission, or SOAE, is another medical theory. This is an emission given off by the inner ear that can cause strange noises, such as the hum.

It appears that the Taos Hum is not such an anomaly after all. Whether it's something in the Earth, or something in the human body, or something in the environment, the hum is not quite as enigmatic as it initially seems. While it might no longer be a mystery, it is certainly an annoyance for those who can hear it.

MARIE LAVEAU

Portrait of Marie Laveau

Born in 1794, Marie Laveau was a Louisiana Creole known as the Voodoo Queen of New Orleans. Laveau was known to heal the sick, rescue condemned men from the gallows, tell fortunes, create potions and charms, and even conduct ceremonies in which the participants would become possessed by voodoo spirits known as loas.

A lot of information on Laveau exists, and much of it is fiction – either made up to enlarge her already massive personality, or fiction meant to smear her name. Separating the truth from the drama has been difficult for a lot of her fans. Following is an account we hope is as accurate as possible. Since most of what is known about the Voodoo

Queen has been passed down orally, it is quite difficult for anyone to say for certain how truthful every piece of information is. Hopefully, the information we have gathered is as close to the truth as it gets.

Laveau was born in the French Quarter on September 10th, 1794, an illegitimate daughter to a wealthy Creole plantation owner and his mistress. She grew up on her father's plantation, was well educated, and a dedicated Catholic who attended mass every single day. As she grew older, she was said to be very beautiful - statuesque, tall, curly black hair, and golden skin. She attracted the attention of a freeperson from Haiti named Jacques Paris, and they were married. Their marriage certificate, containing the names of Marie's parents, is preserved in New Orleans at the St. Louis Cathedral.

In 1824, either by death or desertion, Paris was out of Laveau's life. She then began a career as a hairdresser and part-time nurse, until she entered into a common law marriage with Louis Christoph Dumesnil de Glapion, and began having children by him in succession. Dumesnil was wealthy, so Laveau ended her career to raise her children, which totaled fifteen in all. It was during this period in her life that she became the Voodoo Queen.

Due to the Haitian Revolution of 1804, many Haitians in New Orleans revived the Voodoo religion; and although it was often practiced in the city, it had been banned at different times throughout history due to the sinister connotations people associated with this otherwise peaceful practice. Laveau began to learn the craft from a man calling himself Doctor John, and John Bayou. By 1830, Marie was one of many Voodoo Queens in the area.

But what eventually set Laveau apart were her innovations. She combined Voodoo with many Catholic traditions, such as holy water, incense, Christian prayers, and statues of saints. This combination made the practice of voodoo (the religion) and hoodoo (the magic associated with it) accepted by the upper-class of New Orleans. Laveau believed in spiritual forces that watch over the daily lives of their followers, and can intervene when necessary. Some forces are believed to be kind while others are mischievous. Establishing bonds with these spirits can be achieved through song, dance, music, and even by performing rituals with snakes.

Laveau began performing rituals at the Congo Square, one of the only areas in the segregated section of New Orleans where races could mix. At the Maison Blanche – a house built specifically for voodoo rituals and for rendezvous between black women and white men – Laveau also conducted operations selling gris-gris, charms, and magic powders able to cure certain ailments. She also told fortunes, gave love advice, and would make custom gris-gris based on the customer's desired charms or hexes. Here she would also grant people's wishes and help them by destroying their enemies. Through these operations, she became the true Voodoo Queen of New Orleans.

Once she had overthrown the other queens, she began conducting business behind her cottage on St. Ann Street, performing exorcisms and giving sacrifices to spirits. Though some were critical of her, many feared her, while others revered her. To some, she was a practitioner of black magic and wielder of dark powers, while others thought of her as a saint for humanitarian work – the latter being more accurate.

Ultimately, Laveau retired in 1875, though she continued her humanitarian work with the poor and imprisoned while still offering readings at her home. It was her performing career that was over, as she sought a quieter and more peaceful life. She passed away peacefully on June 18th, 1881 and was buried in the St. Louis Cemetery #1 in the Laveau-Glapion family crypt. The crypt is aboveground, as is required in New Orleans due to the water levels.

Laveau's tomb is the one that attracts the most visitors each year. Another crypt in Cemetery #2, known as the

'Wishing Vault' or 'Voodoo Vault', attracts those who hope Laveau will grant their wishes, and they illegally draw 'xxx' on it to attract her spirit. They also draw pentagrams, hearts, and write poetry and their initials on the white slab as well. Even today, her powerful and impactful legacy lives on as thousands make the pilgrimage to her burial site each year, to pay respects and ask for favors. The legend of the great Marie Laveau may never be forgotten, no matter how much of it remains a mystery.

Marie Laveau's burial site

Plaque on the tomb where Laveau is buried

A better look at the graffiti upon the tomb

Offerings for Marie Laveau, left at her tomb

TAMMY LYNN LEPPERT

Tammy Lynn Leppert

Some of you may not remember the name Tammy Lynn Leppert. She was an actress and model from Cocoa Beach, Florida who had been competing in beauty pageants since the age of four. By the time she was eighteen, with her mother Linda as her agent, she already had the beginnings of an impressive career in film and modeling. She was full of potential stardom. At the age of sixteen, she had been cast in a small role for the 1982 film *Spring Break*. It was a good break for her budding career. But once principle photography for the film had completed, Tammy went to an out-of-town party and was never the same again.

Upon coming home, Tammy behaved curiously. She was withdrawn, paranoid, and acted as though someone were out to harm her. If the phone rang, she asked Wing Flanagan, who was a client of Linda's and had lived with them for years, to answer it and tell whomever it was that she was not home. She even told Wing that she believed the neighbors were spying on her through mirrored windows in their van. When asked about her odd behavior, all she could say was that she had seen things she shouldn't have seen.

Tammy spent nearly two weeks in total seclusion before she landed a very small role in the 1983 classic crime film, *Scarface,* and had a breakdown after the filming of a particularly violent scene. During filming, she stayed with Walter Lebowitz, who was a friend of the family. He visited her after her breakdown and found in her in the throes of a hysterical fit, claiming that someone was going to kill her, and mentioning something about money laundering. She then quit the film and went home.

After returning to Cocoa Beach, she began to improve by seeing a psychiatrist. She was still paranoid, however, and one night she asked Wing to taste her dinner to see if it had been poisoned.

On July 1st, 1983, Tammy stepped outside her home for a moment and when she tried to go back inside, the door had been locked. This sent her into a fit. She picked up a baseball bat and smashed the window in and reached inside to unlock the door. After gaining entry, she found Wing and, believing he had locked her out, began to swing the bat at him. Linda had to intervene and calm Tammy down.

Tammy checked in to the Brevard County Mental Health Center for seventy two hours of observation. While there, doctors could find no evidence of drug or alcohol use and she was released. After leaving the facility, Tammy told Linda that if anything bad happened to her, she wanted Linda to seek revenge because she believed someone was going to kill her.

On July 6th, 1983, Tammy left her home with a friend of hers. They ended up having an argument and Tammy asked to be let out of the car. She got out in the Glass Bank parking lot with no ID, no purse, and no shoes on. She was never seen by anyone who knew her after that.

Tammy's family believes that she had been kidnapped or murdered, based on her previous behavior. She had already informed them that she was going to California for a few weeks, and had no reason to run away. It was suggested that Tammy had been a witness to money laundering and this had caused someone to target her. At the time, there were money laundering investigations taking place in the area, but none have been linked to Tammy Leppert.

Of course, the friend that dropped her off at the Glass Bank parking lot was an initial suspect, but no evidence was ever found to actually connect him to her disappearance. Many people suspected that serial killer Christopher Wilder could have taken and murdered Tammy. He had kidnapped and raped twelve women, murdering eight of them during a crime spree that spanned several states, ending in New Hampshire when he committed suicide while in a struggle with the police. The prevailing theory is that the two of them met on the set of *Scarface* and he began stalking her. Since no evidence to corroborate the suspicion that Tammy was one of his victims has ever surfaced, her disappearance during his spree has been chalked up to coincidence.

The Vampire Rapist, John Crutchley, has been considered a suspect in the case. However, much like the Wilder theory, there is no evidence to support this. Crutchley, though suspected of having murdered as many as thirty women, was never tried or convicted for murder. He was sentenced to life for multiple rape charges; he would drain his victims of so much blood while raping them that they would be on the cusp of death. He died in prison from autoerotic asphyxiation in 2003.

Theories that Tammy had been killed by an ex-boyfriend were later suggested, but again, could never be confirmed. Linda passed in 1995 without any closure. To this day, Tammy Leppert remains missing. She would be fifty-five years old if she is still living at the time of this writing. Perhaps one day the world will know what happened to this rising star. Or, maybe her case will forever remain a mystery.

ELVIS

The King of Rock and Roll, Elvis Presley

Y ou might have read one of our previous books, *Haunts of Hollywood Stars and Starlets*. In it, we give a detailed account of the life and death of Elvis Presley, and the many theories that surround him, regarding ghosts, aliens, faked death, and other conspiracy theories. Perhaps no other celebrity has more mystery surrounding their final days than does the King of Rock and Roll.

Born Elvis Aron Presley on January 8th, 1935 in Tupelo, MS, Elvis came from humble beginnings but would later become one of the most famous cultural icons in the history of the world. He was talented, good looking, and charismatic; fans flocked to see him, battled to touch or even catch a glimpse of him, and when he died on the morning of August 16th, 1977, they mourned him.

His shocking death at his home in Memphis, TN – Graceland – rocked the world. Many fans refused to accept that he was dead, which led to a number of Elvis sightings and the theory that the King had faked his death for a few reasons (to escape fame, to enter the witness protection program). By all accounts, the death seemed accidental, but there are those who believe it was a suicide.

Elvis' stepbrother, Dave Stanley, firmly believes this. At the time of his passing, Elvis was taking many prescription drugs. He had been taking these types of drugs for many years, starting back in 1958 when he joined the military. Over the years, the intake of the drugs increased, and he had a daily regiment by the time he died.

After the King left the Army, he starred in several movies. Though he experienced great commercial success as an actor, starring in musicals and movies that relied on his charm, good looks, and musical talent, he wanted to star in more serious roles, but his management wouldn't allow him. This, combined with the inability to go anywhere without being swarmed, put Elvis in a deep depression, and so he retreated to Graceland to be alone.

He surrounded himself with paid friends who were known as the Memphis Mafia. When he was not touring, he kept himself secluded from the world. This, along with the drug use, ended his six-year marriage to Priscilla. The divorce sent him spiraling further into his melancholy. He became filled with rage and sorrow.

When the late 70s rolled around, Elvis allegedly had to have round-the-clock care because of his severe drug addiction. He was given scheduled doses called "attacks" that were usually mixed with several drugs. He had three doses each day. His diet became incredibly unhealthy, and his caretakers, who were called 'lifers', had to watch him because he would often fall asleep with food in his mouth.

Despite the vast wealth he had once acquired, he was running out of money. He was unhealthy. An upcoming tour filled him with dread. His depression worsened and he lost all will to work, and seemingly live. In the weeks leading up to his death, he became more withdrawn. The last time he saw David, he was crying, and had told his stepbrother goodbye, stating that the next time they met, it would be on a higher plane.

Presley's death came soon after. However, the sequence of events leading up to his passing has never been confirmed. There had been several alterations to his daily routine, including skipping his late night feast and not taking some of his medicines. At 9:30 am, he got up to go to the bathroom and never walked out. When he was found dead in the room, it was discovered that he had taken all three of his attacks at the same time. David believes he did this with the intention of killing himself.

The autopsy stated that the King was dead due to an irregular heartbeat brought about by severe cardiovascular disease, and that there was no evidence to suggest he died of a drug overdose. This finding did not convince his stepbrother, however. Elvis' friend Red West insisted that Presley would not purposely kill himself because of his religious beliefs. Elvis' father, Vernon, had a private autopsy performed on his son, but the results will not be released until the year 2027. Until then, the true nature of Elvis' death will remain a mystery.

AFTERWORD

We sincerely hope you enjoyed this collection of strange and unusual mysteries. While this book is meant to be an entertaining read for those who enjoy such topics, and not in any way meant to be a reference guide or official report, we did make our best efforts to ensure the data we collected was accurate, or at least as accurate as that which exists to the public. Hopefully, for some of these cases, someone might read this book and develop an interest them– an interest that sparks further research. Maybe that research will help uncover the secrets lying beneath the intrigue. If that were to happen, we'd be more than pleased.

This work comes from a lifetime fascination with the unexplained for both of us. As any of you who are familiar with our previous works on both ghosts and aliens, you already know this. You also already know how extensively we research our projects. With just about any of our nonfiction paranormal books, you will find lengthy, detailed bibliographies. This is because we want to be sure to gather as much pertinent information as we can, and also make sure the information exists elsewhere, so as not to include something fabricated or embellished from a single source. Naturally, things might slip through, but it's very difficult for misinformation to pass the many sweeps of our fine-tooth comb.

In case you are wondering about any other cases you think would have been interesting for us to cover, don't worry. There are a lot of stories out there that intrigue us and we are far from through with writing projects, so any story could appear anywhere at any time in any of our books.

We hope you liked the book. We certainly liked writing it. Keep on searching and keep on believing, because the unknown exists around us, and it will remain unknown until someone is curious enough to make it known.

Thank you for joining us. Perhaps we have now helped each other solve a mystery.

-----The Frightening Floyds

Jenny and Jacob Floyd, known as the Frightening Floyds, live in Louisville with their three dogs (Tarzan, Pegasus, and Snow White – a.k.a. BooBoo) and four cats (Baloo, Narnia, Pandy – full name, Pandora Opossum – and Maleficent, whom they call Baby Bat because she looks like a baby bat, and somehow that name has evolved into Bat-Bat, or just simply, The Bat). They enjoy ghosts, aliens, cryptids, traveling, Disney, horror, and a bunch of strange and unusual things. They own and operate Anubis Press, Nightmare Press, Wild West Press, and Poet Tree Grove.

PRAISE FOR
THE FRIGHTENING
FLOYDS

LOUISVILLE'S STRANGE AND UNUSUAL HAUNTS

"This is an amazing book! It's the perfect spooky bedtime read!"

"Some good reading. Enjoyed the stories and history regarding each place."

"...the Floyds do an excellent job at providing the history and stories surrounding the locations in a way that intrigues the reader regardless if they believe in the paranormal or not!"

"From touching the history of the places and the ghost stories/tales around them the book is fantastic... I really hope they get the opportunity to write more."

"This is a great read for anyone who loves the paranormal! Well written and organized!"

"Do you love learning the creepy history of cities?
Do you love getting goosebumps hearing about a good haunting? Then this is the book for you. A fun jaunt through the haunted history of a city with a lot of spooky spots to offer!"

"The history attached with each story is just enough to draw you in."

KENTUCKY'S HAUNTED MANSIONS

"Each mansion features information related to various paranormal activities and events. The authors don't over exaggerate or speak of the paranormal activity as proven fact. They present the material objectively, allowing the reader to decide for themselves. ... Whether a believer or a skeptic, the mansions, their histories, and the facts presented about each home will engage the reader. I was engrossed in every detail about the mansions throughout Kentucky. I love historical buildings and this books was near perfect in feeding my interest."

"The reader is taken on a journey from the hard facts of each mansion, its construction and its various owners and their deeds, through to accounts of paranormal happenings and ghostly sightings. The result is both informative and thoroughly entertaining. The authors are careful not to sensationalise and the narrative comes with a healthy dose of skepticism, leaving it for readers to decide for themselves what to believe. Having experienced the paranormal on numerous occasions I am probably one of the believers, yet this is a book that will appeal just as much to doubters interested in the stories of hauntings and how they have come about. This book is a must read for all who'd like a taste of the history of Kentucky as much as its supernatural inhabitants. As for those after a ghostly tale or two, look no further! This is the sort of book that should be on the shelf of every paranormal writer's bookcase."

OTHER PRAISE

"If you like history and Hollywood then this is the book for you. It was like having a museum at my fingertips." – Amazon Reviewer on *Haunts of Hollywood Stars and Starlets*

"If you love Disney, visiting the parks, and enjoy true ghost stories and legends, this book is the one for you. The Floyds show their love for Disney and don't say the stories they learned are true or not, as they hadn't had experiences, but they don't put the tales down either. Before you head on that Disney vacation, maybe you should pack this book and keep an eye out while on the rides, because maybe that quiet gentleman behind you in line might be something otherworldly." – Pamela K. Kinney, author of *Haunted Richmond, Haunted Richmond II, Virginia's Haunted Historic Triangle, Paranormal Petersburg, Virginia & The Tri-Cities Area, Haunted Virginia: Legends, Myths, & True Tales*, and *Haunted Surry to Suffolk: Spooky Locations Along Routes 10 and 460*, review of *Be Our Ghost*.

BIBLIOGRAPHY

We are always careful to ensure that we have provided information that is as accurate as possible. Of course, we can only access what is available to the public, so with a book such as this, there may be facts regarding missing persons cases and cold cases that we are unable to view. However, we are sure to comb as many sites and sources as possible in the course of our research. For this particular project, interviewing people wasn't really an option. So, we only had what was available online and through libraries to go on. But, as you can see below, we checked and double-checked and cross-referenced numerous sources to acquire the information included in this book. For those of you already familiar with our work, you know well that we are meticulous in our extensive research, and our bibliographies always show it.

So, for further reading on the chapters contained in this book, check the sources below.

Mossbeachdistillery.com

"Speakeasy: Moss Beach Distillery" at mysteryplayground.net

"Is Moss Beach Distillery Haunted?" at seeksghosts.blogspot.com

Riding, Alan (6 April 2005). "In Louvre, New Room With View of 'Mona Lisa'". *The New York Times*. The New York Times Company. Retrieved 7 October 2007

"Mona Lisa – Heidelberger Fund klärt Identität (English: Mona Lisa – Heidelberger find clarifies identity)". University

Library Heidelberg. Archived from the original on 8 May 2011. Retrieved 15 January 2008

Zöllner, Frank (1993). "Leonardo's Portrait of Mona Lisa del Giocondo". *Gazette des Beaux-Arts*. 121 (S): print 115–138. doi:10.11588/artdok.00004207. ISSN 0016-5530.

"The Theft That Made Mona Lisa a Masterpiece". NPR. 30 July 2011. Retrieved 15 February 2019

Lichfield, John (1 April 2005). "The Moving of the Mona Lisa". *The Independent*. Archived from the original on 9 November 2016

Pedretti, Carlo (1982). *Leonardo, a study in chronology and style*. Johnson Reprint Corporation. ISBN 978-0384452800

Vezzosi, Alessandro (2007). "The Gioconda mystery – Leonardo and the 'common vice of painters'". In Vezzosi; Schwarz; Manetti (eds.). *Mona Lisa: Leonardo's hidden face*. Polistampa. ISBN 9788859602583

Lorusso, Salvatore; Natali, Andrea (2015). "Mona Lisa: A comparative evaluation of the different versions and copies". *Conservation Science*. 15: 57–84. Retrieved 26 July 2017

Asmus, John F.; Parfenov, Vadim; Elford, Jessie (28 November 2016). "Seeing double: Leonardo's Mona Lisa twin". *Optical and Quantum Electronics*. 48 (12): 555. doi:10.1007/s11082-016-0799-0

"Highest insurance valuation for a painting". *Guinness World Records*. Retrieved 25 July 2017

Italian: *Prese Lionardo a fare per Francesco del Giocondo il ritratto di mona Lisa sua moglie* Vasari 1879, p.39

Clark, Kenneth (March 1973). "Mona Lisa". The Burlington Magazine (vol 115 ed.). 115(840): 144–151. ISSN 0007-6287. JSTOR 8772

"German experts crack the ID of 'Mona Lisa'". MSN. 14 January 2008. Retrieved 15 January 2008

"Researchers Identify Model for Mona Lisa". *The New York Times* Retrieved 15 January 2008

Kemp, Martin (2006). Leonardo da Vinci: the marvellous works of nature and man. Oxford University Press. ISBN 978-0-19-280725-0. Retrieved 10 October 2010

"D.B. Cooper Hijacking" at fbi.gov

"Bermuda Triangle" at history.com

"Unmasking the Face on Mars" at science.nasa.gov

Sheaffer, Robert. "A Model UFO Debunking". *Skeptical Inquirer, September/October 2007.* Committee for Skeptical Inquiry, Retrieved 15 June 2015

Terence Hines (2003). Pseudoscience and the Paranormal. Prometheus Books, Publishers. pp. 260–. ISBN 978-1-61592-085-3

"Gulf Breeze UFO phenomenon: 30 years later, sightings still divide public" by Troy Moon at pnj.com

"Yeti". Random House Webster's Unabridged Dictionary

Pranavananda, Swami (1957). "The Abominable Snowman". *Journal of the Bombay Natural History Society.* 54.

Stonor, Charles (30 January 1954). *The Statesman in Calcutta*

Swan, Lawrence W. (18 April 1958). "Abominable Snowman". *Science*. 127 (3303): 882–84. Bibcode:1958Sci...127..882S. doi:10.1126/science.127.3303.882-b. PMID 17733822

Stonor, Charles (1955). *The Sherpa and the Snowman*. Hollis and Carter

Straus, William L., Jr. (8 June 1956). "Abominable Snowman". *Science*. 123 (3206): 1024–25. Bibcode:1956Sci...123.1024S. doi:10.1126/science.123.3206.1024. PMID 17800969

Loxton, Daniel; Prothero, Donald R. (2013). Abominable Science!: Origins of the Yeti, Nessie, and Other Famous Cryptids. New York: Columbia University Press. p. 102. ISBN 978-0-231-52681-4

Haviland, Charles (1 December 2007). "'Yeti prints' found near Everest". *BBC News*. Retrieved 1 December 2007

The Bhutan Yeti | Episodes | Destination Truth. Syfy. Retrieved on 7 April 2013.

Lawson, Alastair (25 July 2008). "'Yeti hair' to get DNA analysis". BBC.

'Yeti hairs' belong to a goat By Alastair Lawson – BBC News – 11:20 GMT, Monday, 13 October 2008

"Search for ape man continues against the odds". China.org.cn. 12 October 2010. Retrieved 27 January 2012.

Elder, Miriam (10 October 2011). "Siberia home to Yeti, Bigfoot enthusiasts insist". *The Guardian*. More than a dozen scientists and yeti enthusiasts [...] at a day-long conference [...] "Conference participants came to the conclusion that the artefacts found give 95% evidence of the habitation of the 'snow man' on Kemerovo region territory," the statement said.

"Yeti Evidence Falls Flat: Scientist Says Local Officials Staged Siberian Snowman Hunt For Publicity". Aol.com. Archived from the original on 29 November 2011. Retrieved 27 January 2012.

Izzard, Ralph, *The Abominable Snowman Adventure*, Hodder and Staoughton, 1955.

Taylor, Daniel (1995) *Something Hidden Behind the Ranges: An Himalayan Quest,* San Francisco: Mercury House, ISBN 1562790730.

Tilman, H. W. (1938*) Mount Everest 1938*, Appendix B, pp. 127–37, Pilgrim Publishing. ISBN 81-7769-175-9.

Moore, Robert A. (1983). "The Impossible Voyage of Noah's Ark". *Creation Evolution Journal*. 4 (1): 1–43. Archived from the original on 2016-07-17. Retrieved 2016-07-10

Baring-Gould, Sabine (1884). "Noah". *Legends of the Patriarchs and Prophets and Other Old Testament Characters from Various Sources*. James B. Millar and Co., New York. p. 113.

From a letter written on behalf of Shoghi Effendi, 28 October 1949: *Bahá'í News*, No. 228, February 1950, p. 4. Republished in Compilation 1983, p. 508

Poirier, Brent. "The Kitab-i-Iqan: The key to unsealing the mysteries of the Holy Bible". Archived from the original on 7 July 2011. Retrieved 25 June 2007.

Shoghi Effendi (1971). Messages to the Bahá'í World, 1950–1957. Wilmette, Illinois, USA: Bahá'í Publishing Trust.

p. 104. ISBN 978-0-87743-036-0. Archived from the original on 2008-10-23. Retrieved 2008-08-10.

From a letter written on behalf of Shoghi Effendi to an individual believer, 25 November 1950. Published in Compilation 1983, p. 494

Dyken, JJ (2013*)*. The Divine Default. Algora Publishing. Archived from the original on 2016-07-01. Retrieved 2016-06-23.

"Ark". *Encyclopædia Britannica*. 1. Edinburgh: Society of Gentlemen in Scotland. 1771. Archived from the original on 2018-08-05. Retrieved 2018-06-03.

"Deluge". *Encyclopædia Britannica*. 2. Edinburgh: Society of Gentlemen in Scotland. 1771. Archived from the original on 2018-08-05. Retrieved 2018-06-03.

"Ark". *Encyclopædia Britannica*. 2 Slice 5. Ark: Horace Everett Hooper. 1910. Archived from the original on 2016-03-04. Retrieved 2018-06-03.

"Cameo with Noah's Ark". The Walters Art Museum. Archived from the original on 2013-12-13. Retrieved 2013-12-10.

Fagan, Brian M.; Beck, Charlotte (1996). The Oxford Companion to Archaeology. Oxford: Oxford University Press. ISBN 978-0195076189. Archived from the original on 8 February 2016. Retrieved 17 January 2014.

Feder, Kenneth L. (2010). Encyclopedia of Dubious Archaeology: From Atlantis to the Walam Olum. Santa Barbara, California: ABC-CLIO. ISBN 978-0313379192. Archived from the original on 8 February 2016. Retrieved 17 January 2014.

Mayell, Hillary (27 April 2004). "Noah's Ark Found? Turkey Expedition Planned for Summer". National Geographic Society. Archived from the original on 14 April 2010. Retrieved 29 April 2010.

Stefan Lovgren (2004). Noah's Ark Quest Dead in Water Archived 2012-01-25 at the Wayback Machine – National Geographic

Collins, Lorence G. (2011). "A supposed cast of Noah's ark in eastern Turkey" (PDF). Archived (PDF) from the original on 2016-03-05. Retrieved 2015-10-26

Heise, Kenan (1990). *Resurrection Mary: A Ghost Story*. Chicago Historical Bookworks. ISBN 0-924772-09-3.

Bielski, Ursula (1997). *Chicago Haunts: Ghostlore of the Windy City*. Chicago: Lake Claremont Press.

Chicago Quirk (October 17, 2011). "Meet Chicago's Most Famous Ghost: Resurrection Mary". *Chicago Now.*

"Hunting a Ghost Named Mary". *Chicago Tribune.* October 31, 1985.

Gorner, Peter (May 13, 1974). "Some of Chicago's Favorite Haunts". Chicago Tribune. p. B13.

Geist, Bill (January *31, 1979).* "Cryptic rider leaves taxi driver with the willies". Suburban Trib.

"Killed in Crash". Chicago Tribune. March 12, 1934. p. 5

Bielski, Ursula (March 23, 2007). "Marija: The half-life of Resurrection Mary". GhostVillage.com. Retrieved September 25, 2017

Holub, Joan. *The Haunted States of America ... : Haunted Houses and Spooky Places in All 50 States ... and Canada, too!*. New York, NY: Scholastic Books, 2001.

Kaczmarek, Dale. *Windy City Ghosts*, Ghost Research Society Press, 2005.

"Meet Resurrection Mary, the ghost of Archer Avenue" by Edward McClelland at chicagoreader.com

Joshua Blu Buhs (15 May 2009). Bigfoot: The Life and Times of a Legend. University of Chicago Press. pp. 153–. ISBN 978-0-226-07979-0. Retrieved 7 August 2012.

David J. Daegling (30 October 2004). Bigfoot Exposed: An Anthropologist Examines America's Enduring Legend. Rowman Altamira. pp. 77–. ISBN 978-0-7591-0539-3. Retrieved 7 August 2012.

Michael McLeod (2 June 2009). Anatomy of a Beast: Obsession and Myth on the Trail of Bigfoot. University of California Press. pp. 118–. ISBN 978-0-520-25571-5. Retrieved 7 August 2012.

Hill, Sharon A. "Minnesota Iceman to go back on display (UPDATE: Still hyped as real)". doubtfulnews.com. Retrieved 26 August 2013.

Hill, Sharon A. "Step right up and see the Minnesota Iceman! SOLD!". doubtfulnews.com. Archived from the original on 25 June 2013. Retrieved 26 August 2013.

Austin Daily Herald, July 28th, 1969

"Voodoo Queen of New Orleans" at womenhistoryblog.com

"The Missing Link" by Ivan T. Sanderson from *Argosy Magazine*, May 1969 Issue

"The Strange Story of the Minnesota Ice Man" by Lee Krystek at unmuseum.mus.pa.us

"Defrosting the Minnesota Iceman" by Atomic Mystery Monster at gravediggerslocal.com

"Monster Hunt: Minnesota Iceman" by Katie Heaney at outsideonline.com

"Encino Man: Infamous "Minnesota Iceman" Body Reappears In Texas After Vanishing in 70's" by Greg Newkirk at weekinweird.com

"Minnesota Iceman: Mysterious Frozen Creature from '60s Resurfaces at Museum" by Andy Campbell at huffpost.com

"Thawing the Minnesota Iceman" by Brian Dunning at skeptoid.com

Neanderthal: The Strange Saga of the Minnesota Iceman by Bernard Heuvelmans, translated by Paul LeBlond, with Afterword by Loren Coleman. San Antonio, TX: Anomalist Books, 2016. 284 pp. $22.95 (paperback). ISBN 978-1938398612 – book review from Journal of Scientific Exploration, Vol. 30, No. 4, pp 604-606, 2016

"The Strange Case of the Minnesota Iceman" by Darren Naish at blog.scientificamerican.com

"Minnesota Iceman" by Elle Andra-Warner at northernwilds.com

Strachan, Brady (December 19, 2016). "It could be a lot colder: Kelowna historian remembers Okanagan Lake freezing over completely". CBC.

Orkin, Mark M. 2015 [1971]. Speaking Canadian English: An Informal Account of the English Language in Canada, p. 205. Routledge. ISBN 1317436334

Radford, Benjamin; Nickell, Joe (May 5, 2006). Lake Monster Mysteries: Investigating the World's Most Elusive Creatures. USA: University Press of Kentucky. p. 117. ISBN 978-0813123943.

Radford, Benjamin; Nickell, Joe (May 5, 2006). Lake Monster Mysteries: Investigating the World's Most Elusive Creatures. *USA*: University Press of Kentucky. pp. 12-125. ISBN 978-0813123943.

"Literacy, Transformation and Naitaka (Ogopogo)". *Sean Dyer's Canadian Literature Blog English* 470.

Radford, Benjamin; Nickell, Joe (May 5, 2006). Lake Monster Mysteries: Investigating the World's Most Elusive Creatures. USA: University Press of Kentucky. p. 121. ISBN 978-0813123943.

Radford, Benjamin; Nickell, Joe (May 5, 2006). Lake Monster Mysteries: Investigating the World's Most Elusive Creatures. USA: University Press of Kentucky. p. 113. ISBN 978-0813123943.

"Parks Canada - News Releases and Backgrounders". *web.archive.org*. March 6, 2017. Archived from the original on 2017-03-06.

Radford, Benjamin; Nickell, Joe (May 5, 2006). Lake Monster Mysteries: Investigating the World's Most Elusive Creatures. *USA*: University Press of Kentucky. p. 119. ISBN 978-0813123943.

Radford, Benjamin. "Ogopogo: Canada's Loch Ness Monster". *Live Science*. Retrieved July 13, 2015.

Kadane, Lisa. "Canada's mysterious lake monster". www.bbc.com. Retrieved 2020-03-16.

Radford, Benjamin; Nickell, Joe (May 5, 2006). Lake Monster Mysteries: Investigating the World's Most Elusive Creatures. USA: University Press of Kentucky. p. 118. ISBN 978-0813123943.

Radford, Benjamin; Nickell, Joe (May 5, 2006). Lake Monster Mysteries: Investigating the World's Most Elusive Creatures. USA: University Press of Kentucky. pp. 119-120. ISBN 978-0813123943.

"Canada's Loch Ness Monster Captured on Video?". Discovery News. November 14, 2011. Retrieved November 15, 2011.

"Canada's Loch Ness Monster Captured on Video?". Fox News. November 14, 2011. Retrieved February 7, 2020.

O'Neill, Marnie (October 5, 2018). "Canada's Loch Ness Monster, the legendary Ogopogo lake monster, caught on video". Fox News. Retrieved October 6, 2018.

Radford, Benjamin. "Ogopogo the Chameleon". The Committee for Skeptical Inquiry. Center for Inquiry. Archived from the original on March 4, 2016. Retrieved July 13, 2015.

Radford, Benjamin. "Ogopogo: Canada's Loch Ness Monster". livescience.com. Live Science. Retrieved 20 May 2019.

Radford, Ben; Nickell, Joe (May 2006). Lake Monster Mysteries: Investigating the World's Most Elusive Creatures. University Press of Kentucky. ASIN B0078XFQKQ.

Jan 19, Grant Scott-; Story: 69920, 2012 / 10:58 am |. "Waterspouts visible for miles - West Kelowna News". www.castanet.net.

Gaal, Arlene (2001) *In Search of Ogopogo*. Hancock House, Surrey, British Columbia

Gaal, Arlene (1986) *Ogopogo: The True Story of The Okanagan Lake Million Dollar Monster*. Hancock House, Surrey, BC.

Moon, Mary (1977) *Ogopogo*. Douglas Ltd., North Vancouver, British Columbia.

Nickell, Joe (2006) "Ogopogo: The Lake Okangan Monster". *Skeptical Inquirer*, 30(1): 16–19.

Radford, Benjamin (2006) "Ogopogo the Chameleon". *Skeptical Inquirer*, 30(1): 41–46.

Radford, Benjamin and Nickell, Joe (2006) *Lake Monster Mysteries: Investigating the World's Most Elusive Creatures*. University Press of Kentucky, Lexington, Kentucky.

Salmonson, Jessica Amanda (1992) *The Mysterious Doom and Other Ghostly Tales of the Pacific Northwest: 149*. Sasquatch Books, Seattle, Washington.

"OGOPOGO - The Okanagan's Friendly Lake Monster TRUTH OR FICTION?" at Okanagan.com

"Legend of Ogopogo" at tourismkelowna.com

"Man Releases 18-Year-Old Pictures of 'Ogopogo', Canada's Lake Monster" at cryptozoologynews.com

"The July 11th, 1991 Mexico City UFOs: Basic Astronomy Ignored" by Tim Printy at astronomyufo.com

"6 UFO Hotspots Around the World" by Frances Romero at content.time.com

"Parishioners Say Statue Closed Its Eyes" by Sheila Mullan at upi.com

"Artist Calls Crucifix Eye Closing Divine" by Tim Vercillotti from *The Pittsburgh Press*, March 28th, 1989, page 6

"Thousands Visit Church Where Crucifix Closed Its Eyes" by Tara Bradley-Steck, April 1st, 1989, *Associated Press*

"Hundreds Going to See Crucifix Trinity Roman Catholic Church in Ambridge, Pa." April 2nd, 1989. *Tulsa World*. Retrieved at tulsaworld.com

"Looking For a Miracle In Closed Eyes" by John M. Baer, April 9th, 1989. *Washing Post*. Retrieved at washingtonpost.com

"Panel: Crucifix Didn't Blink" from *Pittsburgh Post Gazette*, published July 6th, 1989, page 1; retrieved at newspapers.com

"'Miracle in Ambridge' Church Pastor Resigns" from *Pittsburgh Post Gazette*, published August 14th, 1989, page 1; retrieved at newspapers.com

"'Miracle' Pastor Resigns" (August 14th, 1989) from *UPI Archives* at upi.com

"Religion: 'Miracle' Pastor Resigns" (August 14th, 1989) at latimes.com

"With 'Miracle' Discounted, Mill Town Pastor Resigns" atwashingtonpost.com

"It's a Miracle" by Andrew Johnson at archive.triblive.com

"Cvitkovic, OFM, Fr. Vincent" obituary, August 8th, 2004, from the *Chicago Tribune*

"Domenic J. Leo, Sr." obituary, at darrochfuneralhome.com

"Rec. ITU-R V.431-7, Nomenclature of the frequency and wavelength bands used in telecommunications" (PDF). ITU. Archived from the original (PDF) on 31 October 2013. Retrieved 20 February 2013.

"Extremely Low Frequency". *ANL Glossary*. NASA. Retrieved 28 September 2013.

"Extremely low frequency". *ANL Glossary*. Archived from the original on 29 October 2013. Retrieved 9 August 2011.

Liemohn, Michael W. and A. A. CHAN, "Unraveling the Causes of Radiation Belt Enhancements Archived 27 May 2010 at the Wayback Machine". EOS, TRANSACTIONS, AMERICAN GEOPHYSICAL UNION, Volume 88, Number 42, 16 October 2007, pages 427-440. Republished by NASA and accessed online, 8 February 2010. Adobe File, page 2.

Barr, R.; Jones, D. Llanwyn; Rodger, C. J. (2000). "ELF and VLF radio waves". Journal of Atmospheric and Solar-Terrestrial Physics. 62 (17–18): 1689–1718. Bibcode:2000JASTP..62.1689B. doi:10.1016/S1364-6826(00)00121-8.

"Extremely Low Frequency Transmitter Site, Clam Lake, Wisconsin" (PDF). *Navy Fact File*. United States Navy. 28 June 2001. Retrieved 17 February 2012. at the Federation of American Scientists website

Wolkoff, E. A.; W. A. Kraimer (May 1993). "Pattern Measurements of U.S. Navy ELF Antennas" (PDF). *ELF/VLF/LF Radio Propagation and Systems Aspects*. Belgium: AGARD Conference proceedings 28 Sept. – 2 Oct. 1992, NATO. pp. 26.1–26.10. Retrieved 17 February 2012.

Coe, Lewis (2006). Wireless Radio: A brief history. USA: McFarland. pp. 143–144. ISBN 978-0786426621.

Sterling, Christopher H. (2008). Military communications: from ancient times to the 21st century. ABC-CLIO. pp. 431–432. ISBN 978-1851097326.

Bashkuev, Yu. B.; V. B. Khaptanov; A. V. Khankharaev (December 2003). "Analysis of Propagation Conditions of ELF Radio Waves on the "Zeus"–Transbaikalia Path". Radiophysics and Quantum Electronics. 46 (12): 909-917. Bibcode:2003R&QE...46..909B. doi:10.1023/B:RAQE. 0000029585.02723.11.

Jacobsen, Trond (2001). "ZEVS, The Russian 82 Hz ELF Transmitter". Radio Waves Below 22 kHz. Renato Romero webpage. Retrieved 17 February 2012.

Hardy, James (28 February 2013). "India makes headway with ELF site construction". IHS Jane's Defence Weekly. Archived from the original on 23 February 2014. Retrieved 23 February 2014.

"Navy gets new facility to communicate with nuclear submarines prowling underwater". The Times of India. 31 July 2014.

https://www.thedrive.com/the-war-zone/25728/chinas-new-york-city-sized-earthquake-warning-system-sounds-more-like-way-to-talk-to-subs

"U.S. Navy: Vision...Presence...Power." SENSORS - Subsurface Sensors. US Navy. Accessed 7 February 2010.

G, Gary. "Windsor Hum". The Windsor-Essex County Hum. Retrieved March 26, 2019.

"Have you heard 'the Hum'?". BBC News. 19 May 2009.

https://www.youtube.com/watch?v=QpeKot2X_O8

"What's that terrible noise?". *The Independent*. 22 June 1994.

"Expert has the answer to Woodland village hums". The Advertiser Series. 23 August 2011.

Baguley, David; Andersson, Gerhard; McFerran, Don; McKenna, Laurence (2013*)*. Tinnitus: A Multidisciplinary Approach. Wiley-Blackwell. p. 244. ISBN 978-1-86156-403-0.

"In Taos, Researchers Can Hum It, but They Can't Name That Sound". LA Times. 1 September 1993.

"Scientists Track Down Source of Earth's Hum" by Hadley Leggett at wired.com

Fandrich, Ina J. (2005). "The Birth of New Orleans' Voodoo Queen: A Long-Held Mystery Resolved". *Louisiana History: The Journal of the Louisiana Historical Association*. 46 (3): 293–309. JSTOR 4234122.

Marie Laveau the Mysterious Voudou Queen: A Study of Powerful Female Leadership in Nineteenth-Century New Orleans by Ina Johanna Fandrich

Loustaunau, Martha, Denmke. Marie Laveau. Salem Press Enclycopedia. p. 1. Retrieved 9 February 2015.

"Marie Laveau: Separating fact from fiction about New Orleans' Voodoo queen". *NOLA.com*. Retrieved 2018-07-06.

"Dictionary of Louisiana Biography - L - Louisiana Historical Association". www.*lahistory.org*. Retrieved 2018-07-07.

Vitelli, Dr. Romeo. "The Marie Laveau Phenomenon". *archive.randi.org*. Retrieved 2018-07-06.

Tallant, Robert (1946). *Voodoo in New Orleans (1984 reprint)*. New York: Macmillan Company - reprint Pelican Publishing. ISBN 978-0-88289-336-5.

Morrow., Long, Carolyn (2006). *A New Orleans voudou priestess : the legend and reality of Marie Laveau*. Gainesville: University Press of Florida. ISBN 0813029740. OCLC 70292161.

Vitelli, Dr. Romeo. "The Marie Laveau Phenomenon". *archive.randi.org*. Retrieved 2018-07-08.

Ward, Martha. *Voodoo Queen: The Spirited Lives of Marie Laveau* (Jackson: University Press of Mississippi, 2004).

Carolyn Morrow Long: *A New Orleans Voudou Priestess: The Legend and Reality of Marie Laveau*, 2018

Long, Carolyn Morrow (2005). "Marie Laveau: A Nineteenth-Century Voudou Priestess". *Louisiana History: The Journal of the Louisiana Historical Association*. 46 (3): 262–292. JSTOR 4234121.

Duggal, Barbra Rosendale (2000). Creole, *The History and Legacy of Louisiana's Free People of Color*. Baton Rouge: Louisiana State University Press. pp. 157–178.

Long, Carolyn Morrow. *A New Orleans Voudou Priestess: The Legend and Reality of Marie Laveau*, Gainesville: University Press of Florida (2006), (ISBN 9780813029740).

"Voodoo Queen Marie Laveau's tomb in New Orleans, LA (Google Maps)". *Virtual Globetrotting*. 2014-09-10. Retrieved 2018-07-12.

Webster, Richard A. (December 30, 2013). "Repair of Marie Laveau's tomb to take months, potential suspect attempted to paint another tomb one month ago". The New Orleans Times-Picayune. Retrieved 2014-01-05.

"When the Misfits got arrested in a New Orleans cemetery: a 1982 story from our crypt". Retrieved 22 January 2017.

Webster, Richard A. (January 2, 2014). "Marie Laveau's tomb suffering significant damage during restoration process, nonprofit says". The New Orleans Times-Picayune. Retrieved 2014-01-05. But when Angie Green, executive director of Save Our Cemeteries, a nonprofit group that works to preserve historic cemeteries throughout the city, saw someone blasting Laveau's tomb with a high-pressure water gun she said she immediately called the Archdiocese. "Pressure washing is terrible for any old building," Green said. "When I first saw them doing it they had two sides done and there were chips of brick and plaster from the tomb all over the ground. I asked them to stop and everyone (at the Archdiocese) said they would stop but they are still doing it." [Sarah McDonald, director of communications for the Archdiocese,] said Green's allegation that the pressure washing is inflicting significant damage is "inaccurate."

"Grave disquiet; Briefs." Irish Independent. (January 29, 2015 Thursday): 64 words. LexisNexis Academic. Web. Date Accessed: 2015/02/12.

Dessens, Nathalie (2008). "Reviewed Work: A New Orleans Voudou Priestess: The Legend and Reality of Marie Laveau by Carolyn Morrow Long". *Caribbean Studies*. 36 (1): 166–170. doi:10.1353/crb.0.0008. JSTOR 25613150.

North, Bill (January 2003). *...to build up a rich collection...:Selected Works From the Marianna Kistler Beach Museum of Art*. Marianna Kistler Beach Museum of Art. p. 110. ISBN 1-890751-11-1.

Rose, Al (1987). *I Remember Jazz: Six Decades Among the Great Jazzmen*. Baton Rouge and London: LSU Press. p. 7. ISBN 0-8071-2571-7.

My missing sister Tammy Leppert at https://www.facebook.com/findtammyleppert/ (@findtammyleppert)

"What Happend To Tammy Leppert??". Archived from the original on October 27, 2009. Retrieved 8 July 2015.

"Tammy Lynn Leppert: Biography". IMDb. Retrieved 2016-09-09.

LYNN LEPPERT Retrieved on 16 Jan 2018

"NamUs MP # 1376". *findthemissing.org*. National Missing and Unidentified Persons System. 20 January 2009. Retrieved 8 July 2015.

"Tammy Leppert". *missingkids.org*. National Center for Missing & Exploited Children. Retrieved 8 July 2015.

Florida Today Cocoa, Florida Saturday, November 30, 1985 - Page 5A

"Tammy Lynn Leppert" at *The Charley Project* at charleyproject.org

"Case File 211DFFL" at doenetork.org

"1983 Leppert, Tammy Lynn July 6, 1983" at *Porchlight USA* at tapatalk.com

"7 years ago, model says goodbye, hasn't been seen since" from *Florida Today*, Sunday, March 18, 1990, page 38; retrieved at newspapers.com

"The Missing Beauty Queen – Tammy Lynn Leppert" by Emily Thompson at morbidology.com

Baden, Michael M.; Hennessee, Judith Adler. *Unnatural Death: Confessions of a Medical Examiner*. Ballantine; 1990. ISBN 0-8041-0599-5.

Bouchard, Dany. "Priscilla Presley Keeps King Alive". *Toronto Sun*. November 5, 2010; Retrieved November 9, 2010

Brown, Peter Harry; Broeske, Pat H. *Down at the End of Lonely Street: The Life and Death of Elvis Presley*. Signet; 1997. ISBN 0-451-19094-7.

Clarke, Steve. "Conspiracy Theories and Conspiracy Theorizing". In: Coady, David, editor. *Conspiracy Theories: The Philosophical Debate*. Ashgate; 2006. ISBN 0-7546-5250-5.

Clayton, Dick; Heard, James. *Elvis: By Those Who Knew Him Best*. Virgin Publishing; 2003. ISBN 0-7535-0835-4.

CNN. Elvis Presley Fast Facts; May 12, 2017; Retrieved January 20, 2018

Connelly, Charlie. *In Search of Elvis: A Journey to Find the Man Beneath the Jumpsuit*. Little, Brown; 2008. ISBN 0-349-11900-7

Fensch, Thomas. *The FBI Files on Elvis Presley*. New Century Books; 2001. ISBN 0-930751-03-5.

The Guardian. "Channel 4 Show 'Discovers Cause of Elvis Presley's Death'"; March 25, 2014; Retrieved January 20, 2018.

Hopkins, Jerry. *Elvis: The Final Years*. Berkley; 1986. ISBN 0-425-08999-1.

Hopkins, Jerry. *Elvis—The Biography*. Plexus; 2007. ISBN 0-85965-391-9.

Keogh, Pamela Clarke. Elvis Presley: The Man, The Life, The Legend. Simon & Schuster; 2004. ISBN 0-7434-5603-3

Mason, Bobbie Ann. Elvis Presley. Penguin; 2007. ISBN 0-14-303889-3.

Nash, Alanna, et al. *Elvis and the Memphis Mafia*. Aurum; 2005. ISBN 1-84513-128-2.

"Long Live the King". *The New York Times*. August 16, 2002; Retrieved December 30, 2009.

Ponce de Leon, Charles L. *Fortunate Son: The Life of Elvis Presley*. Macmillan; 2007. ISBN 0-8090-1641-9.

Presley, Priscilla. *Elvis and Me*. G.P. Putnam's Sons; 1985. ISBN 0-399-12984-7.

Ramsland, Katherine. TruTV. "Cyril Wecht: Forensic Pathologist—Coverup for a King"; 2010 archived November 5, 2013.

Stanley, David; Coffey, Frank. *The Elvis Encyclopedia*. Virgin Books; 1998. ISBN 0-7535-0293-3.

Tennant, Forest. "Elvis Presley: Head Trauma, Autoimmunity, Pain, and Early Death". *Practical Pain Management*. June 2013; Retrieved January 9, 2018.

Everct, Todd. Variety. Elvis Presley, 42, Found Dead in His Memphis Mansion; August 17, 1977; Retrieved September 21, 2018

PHOTOGRAPH CREDITS

01: Moss Beach Distillery by Krista, from Flickr
02: Moss Beach Distillery from Wikimedia Commons
03: Moss Beach Distillery by Kim Scarborough, from Flickr
04: Mona Lisa painting by Leonardo Da Vinci, work is public domain
05: D.B. Cooper FBI sketch with age progression, from Wikimedia Commons
06: D.B. Cooper FBI Bulletin for D.B. Cooper, from Wikimedia Commons
07: D.B. Cooper, Richard McCoy Jr. – the strongest lead the FBI has had, from Wikimedia Commons
08: Bermuda Triangle from Flickr
09: Face on Mars original photo from Wikimedia Commons
10: Face on Mars highest resolution photo from NASA Jet Propulsion Laboratory
11: Gulf Breeze UFO drawing, Wikimedia Commons
12: Ogopogo statue, from Wikimedia Commons
13: Drawing of the Yeti, free picture by Pixabay
14: Yeti footprint from Wikipedia
15: Yeti tracks with what is believed to be a Yeti in the distance, from Wikipedia
16: Mound in Turkey some believe to be Noah's Ark, from Wikimedia Commons
17: Another view of the mound in Turkey believed to be Noah's Ark, from Wikipedia
18: Mt. Ararat in Turkey, sight of another location believed to hold Noah's Ark within a glacier, from Wikipedia
19: Resurrection Cemetery, front gates, from Wikimedia Commons
20: Drawing of the Minnesota Iceman, from Wikimedia Commons
21: Portrait of Marie Laveau, from Wikimedia Commons
22: Marie Laveau's tomb in New Orleans, LA, from Flickr
23: Commemorative plaque on the grave of Marie Laveau, from Wikimedia Commons
24: Another look at Marie Laveau's tomb to see all the graffiti, free picture at Pixabay
25: Offerings at the tomb of Marie Laveau, from Wikimedia Commons
26: A picture of Tammy Lynn Leppert, from Wikimedia Commons
27: Elvis, from Flickr

SOME SAMPLES
FROM OTHER
ANUBIS PRESS BOOKS
TO CHECK OUT

From

AMERICAN CRYPTIC

by Jim Towns

Myths and fables (and yes even ghost stories) enjoy a particular longevity because they're malleable, and can be reshaped to fit this individual context of their storyteller, free of the burden of facts and dates and, god forbid, truth. This makes them both powerful, and like any powerful thing, potentially dangerous. Folk tales can oftentimes dress themselves up as truth, or history, but they have a very different purpose. Rather than to purely inform, their intent is to elicit a specific reaction in the listener or reader: like awe, or pride, or terror. And the strongest of these stories affect us not just on an intellectual level, but a physical one as well. A stirring speech can move its audience to cheers...or anger. A powerful folk story can bring tears, and any good ghost story gives its audience a chill up the spine.

Because there's intellectual truth, and then there's emotional truth- and they are frequently not the same thing.

Maybe the most interesting part of this work for me was discovering the truth behind some of these stories, and comparing it to the legend to see how much overlap the two have- how easily they share the same space. The things I learned are mostly included in the preceding stories, mainly that in order for history to become myth, it usually has to be whittled away at, until the story is just a basic framework onto which each successive storyteller can hang their own chosen dressing. In this whittling process we lose much of what was true or real, but what's gained is a new narrative versatility, which allows the story to go on and on, changing a little bit with each telling- like a game of telephone - a living, evolving thing that can potentially live forever. Not a hundred-percent real, but not entirely fabricated, either. A shadowy thing lurking in the mind or on the shelves, waiting to steal our attention away for a few moments, in order to fulfill some basic need we humans have to be thrilled, or moved, or even just distracted.

We each tell our own stories, and in doing so, we each perform our own unique magic upon our audience, whether it's across the flickering flames of a campfire, in ten-point typeset on a faded white page, or a small glowing screen in the dark. The stories we share unite us, and remind us we're all part of a larger narrative that goes on, and on.

FROM
HAUNTED SURRY TO SUFFOLK:
SPOOKY LOCATIONS ALONE
ROUTES 10 AND 460
by Pamela K. Kinney

Excerpt from "Haunts and Legends of The Great Dismal Swamp" chapter *of Haunted Surry to Suffolk: Spooky Tales Along Routes 10 and 460.*

AUTHOR'S VISIT AND INVESTIGATION NOVEMBER 17, 2019

We returned on Sunday, November 17, 2019. It must have rained the night before as everything looked wet, and it was colder than the previous day, although the wind was not as bad. Many trees had taken on the costume of autumn, with various colors, and the gray, cloudy skies gave an aura of spookiness not there back in April. This time, the center was closed, so we couldn't stop there. We drove down the same road we had taken back in April, but we stopped at the sign that required us to purchase a permit to be allowed to drive our car down to Lake Drummond. Of course, not having enough change and no checks, I ended up doing a ghost box and EVP session there before taking some pictures.

I turned both the recorder and the ghost box on, setting the latter to scanning radio stations.

"Are there any spirits here in Dismal Swamp?"

"Who is connected to the Underground Railroad I see happened here? Anyone who became part of the maroon colony here?"

"Is the bride and her husband who'd been seen by a park ranger still haunting here? Any Colonial spirits here?"

"Philip," a male voice uttered from my ghost box.

A woman also replied, "Colton."

"First name?"

She said, "Fran."

Again, the male said, "Philip."

"How many spirits are here right now?"

A male voice said, "10."

But not actually hearing that at the time and thinking I heard nine, I asked if it was nine, and the same spirit said, "No!" (I heard all this better in the quiet of my home, off the laptop, and with headphones).

"Any ghost here connected to that slave rebellion that happened around here, where many white people were killed?"

A male voice uttered, "Bleed."

"Are any natives here, of local tribes?" I didn't get any answer to that, but again, this might be due to them not understanding English.

I attempted something else. "Have you seen pirates around here back when you were alive? Like Blackbeard?"

Nothing.

"Any ghosts here?"

A male voice said, "Yes." Then, I got, "John. Philip."

I said, "Dismal Swamp looks haunted to me."

What sounded like the same male voice replied, "It is."

"Anybody died here and is buried in the swamp?"

I got, "Three."

I said, "Goodbye. I'm leaving now, so don't follow me home, please. Good day."

A man called out from the box. "Goodbye."

I did a quick EVP session after I shut off the box. I asked several questions, but only one got me an EVP. I inquired if anyone had drowned in Lake Drummond and I did get "Lake Drummond."

We drove to the Washington Ditch Canal and drove down the road to the parking lot. I grabbed the ghost box and recorder and slung my camera around my neck, leaving Bill in the car.

I read the signs I saw there, taking pictures of them. One mentioned Washington Ditch and said: "Surveyed by George Washington in 1763. A cart road was built along this 4 ½ mile ditch, and the canal dug alongside by slave labor for transportation. Gresham Nimmo, under the personal direction of George Washington, did the surveying and kept the notes."

The other was about Dismal Town. It said, "Washington and company used this spot as their Dismal Swamp headquarters. The town was built prior to the Nimmo Survey of 1763 on Riddick 402 Acre Patent."

Now there is a word here that would come up three times in my ghost box session. At the time, I heard it and thought of the family who had it as their last name whose house was in Suffolk, but after listening to the recordings and looking at the picture, it was clear what the ghosts were trying to say.

I turned on both the ghost box and recorder, and I began.

"Any spirits here?"

Something answered but spoke too low.

"Names?"

"Riddick."

"Washington and company? George Washington?"

"Riddick." Second time for that word.

"Are there any spirits of slaves here? Connected to here or the swamp?"

A female voice from my box said, "Dug." (With slaves digging the canal, I understood later when I was home that this was a slave who dug the canal).

"Why are you still here?"

Something answered, but again too low.

"Do you feel you're stuck to this land?"

"Marked."

"Names?"

Once again, I got the word, "Riddick."

I said, "I am going now. Goodbye. Good day."

A male voice from my box uttered, "Good day."

I switched off the ghost box and the recorder, before hurrying back to the car. We still had two places in downtown historic Suffolk to investigate, and it was already 3:00 p.m. I needed to get home to eat and get all the audio and pictures uploaded.

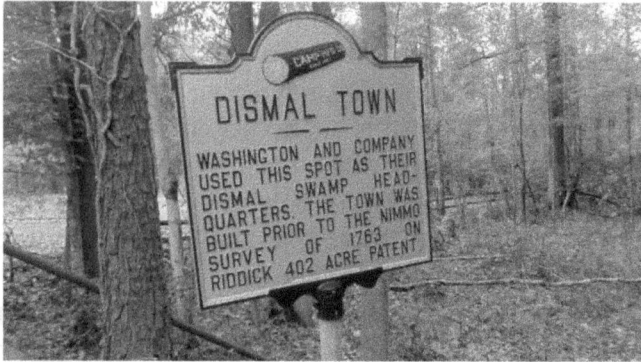

The word Riddick came over three times through my ghost box, and it hit me what the spirits were telling me after looking at the sign in this photo.

Those who live in the area and tourists who visit claim they see wispy white things, especially around the lake, but no doubt what they saw could be foxfire, a substance given off when certain fungi decay wood. Again, maybe they did see something. The place can be eerie, especially if shrouded in fog or mist. And besides spirits, you might run into Bigfoot or fairies. Do take care and don't strike out alone in the woods and head off the designated trails, for you never know who or what you might meet. You might encounter more than animals and birds in the Great Dismal Swamp, and the haunts and Bigfoot are waiting to welcome you, even if it means taking the portal to Hell.

There are two Bacon's Castle excerpts from the chapter. One talks about the ghost stories and legends, other is my own experiences during the ghost tour they hold each October.

Bacon's Castle is the oldest building in America, with the oldest formal English garden, too, and is a rare example of American Jacobean architecture. It is the only surviving "high-style" house in the nation from the 17th century. It is one of only three surviving Jacobean great homes in the Western Hemisphere—the other two are in Barbados. It has the oldest formal English garden in North America and is listed on the National Register of Historic Places and was designated as a National Historic Landmark in 1960.

There is one love story with Bacon's Castle that can't be proven, and so might be a myth. A young woman in the 1800s met her lover, a farmer, in secret on the side of a cornfield. Her father didn't approve of him. But when she had returned to Bacon's Castle one evening, carrying a candle upstairs to her room, she tripped, and her long hair caught fire from the candle flame. Not wanting her father to know she had been out, she kept quiet and ran from the house, back to the cornfield and her lover. She died in his arms, severely burned.

Bacon's Castle is rife with hauntings, and there are those who say it is the work of the Devil. Someone in connection with another historical building and cemetery, whose wife works at the house, told me a story about some paranormal investigators who had recorded an EVP of a diabolical laugh and voice in the basement (where the large fireplace is). He believes it to be the Devil himself. Others hold the belief that it is the return of Nathaniel Bacon's men. Although it's unlikely that every historic building in Virginia is haunted, there are several that have an undeniably eerie allure to them—like Bacon's Castle. And let's be honest, with so many years of people living there, it could even be members of families who owned the house, slaves, and much more.

Paranormal investigators who have investigated there believe that many of the disembodied spirits are those of the slaves who were subjected to unbearable living conditions. While the mansion was decorated lavishly, the slave quarters hardly had any furniture at all. In place of beds, servants were expected to sleep on piles of hay and rags.

Whatever the spirits may be from, there are numerous sightings, from moaning in the attic to strange noises, floating heads, and unseen entities passing by. The one about the fireball is interesting.

Seen as a pulsating, red ball of fire, it rises from the graveyard of Olde Lawne's Creek Church, which is south of Bacon's Castle. It soars to the castle grounds, "floating or hovering" there before heading back to the Olde Lawne's Creek Church graveyard to vanish.

There were reports of sightings of this fireball over the years. What can it be? Skeptics say it can be explained, while others call it a manifestation of the Devil. One legend tells of a servant a century or two ago, late doing his chores. As he walked home in the dark, a red object appeared out of nowhere and burst, covering him in flames and burning him to death.

Another story talks about hidden money in the castle and that two men had found it years ago while removing some bricks in the fireplace hearth in the second floor's west room. No one had ever found the money, and no one has seen the light since.

Excerpt from Bacon's Castle chapter- "AUTHOR'S EXPERIENCES DURING

GHOST TOUR OF BACON'S CASTLE OCTOBER 2017

I paid to take the ghost tour of the building on October 2, 2016, led by members of the Center for Paranormal Research and Investigations (CPRI).

I walked over to the left side of the house, which was the original section, and started my ghost box up. I began asking questions to see if I would get any answers.

"Is Nathaniel Bacon here at the Allen House?"

A man's voice spoke from my box. "No. He was never here."

Well, that is accurate.

"Are you one of Bacon's men who took over the house? Are you the only one still here in spirit?"

"Yes. There are others."

After that, my battery died, so I took the box and recorder back to the car where Bill waited. I handed both to him and got one of my mini camcorders, but I found the new battery I placed in it had already died. Well, CPRI claims this place is the most haunted in Virginia they ever encountered.

On my way out of the restroom on the newer section of the house I realized I'd not shut the door all the way, so I turned halfway around, when the door closed itself, smacking me lightly on the rear end. I double-checked through a downstairs window to the right of the door, where the investigators were, but I saw no one had left that room, as neither did anyone from the workers' office. Had one of the spirits been upset I hadn't shut the door as was proper, so they did it themselves? I can't verify that for sure, but it did happen, and I was quick enough to look through that window, which gave me a great vantage point to see if a living person had done it.

People began lining up, so I hustled over to join them. Our guide was one of the investigators from CPRI, and he led us around back of the Allen manor to a place that may have been where the slaves lived. He talked about the history of it as well as their findings after they'd investigated the place before he took us inside the main house.

He led us into the older section of the place. It was highly unusual for a home like that, as no others of that kind of building were around at that time. The first room we entered might have been used for entertainment. The guide said he couldn't be sure if the past residents played cards in there, but they had used it for socializing. There had been disembodied voices and unexplained sounds heard in there, even by the paranormal group live or on recordings. People claimed that a chair moved in there, for they would always find it in a different spot where they had left it whenever they returned to the room. The group always marked the chair to see if it moved, but it hadn't the past few years. They had something attached beneath it to catch any sounds if it did move. I asked if they ever had someone sit in the chair and wait to see if it moved, but he admitted that they never thought to do that.

He pointed out that the windows had etchings and markings on the glass, like drawings and writing from past occupants of the Allen house spanning a hundred years. Also, the furnishings in the room were not original to that era, although there were some rooms upstairs that had actual furniture used in that period.

The guide then led us down a flight of stairs to the basement where the kitchen was. Once down there, I asked if any spirits were with us and if they could say something into the small digital camcorder I held. I used it instead of a recorder, to capture EVPs as much as video. Later, I uploaded it and listened, but got nothing.

This kitchen is unusual for a southern house in that period, for they usually kept the kitchen in a building outside the main house. Slaves cooked out there and brought in the food to the dining room at mealtimes. But in Bacon's Castle, there is a massive fireplace where they did the cooking. Our guide pointed out that where there is a wall now, there'd once been a door on the left. It must have kept the upstairs warm in the wintertime. They also had their own wine. Now, it is made again and sold in reproduction bottles of the Allen wine.

Our guide pointed out the cross beams in the ceiling and that the wood all around us was the original material from that time. Very remarkable as many historic homes in Virginia had replaced many of their wooden floors and walls by the 21st century. He also pointed out a creepy black shadow on a wall, but it was nothing paranormal, but was caused by soot or something similar. It did look like a figure.

He mentioned that people had heard voices and noises where we stood. We were told to remain silent for a few minutes to see if we heard anything. Suddenly, I could hear voices from a room above us, followed by a scraping sound.

Our guide said, "Did anyone else hear that besides me? That sounds like it came from the room where the chair is— the scraping would be the chair moving."

Most raised their hands or said they did hear the sound, just as I did.

Because I know I heard voices before the chair movement, I asked, "Is there another tour group up there, maybe? Can you check?"

He called over on his radio, "Anyone in the older section beside us?"

He couldn't get anyone, as for some reason, his walkie-talkie wouldn't work. Was it due to the paranormal or just ordinary reasons?

Later, when I listened to the recording, I heard the faint voices and the scraping afterward. So, I had caught something, proving I had heard the voices, and not just the chair! Also after the tour had finished, I asked him to let me know by email if there had been a group of living people in that room, as I said I was sure I heard voices beforehand. When I got an email from him, he stated we were the only group in that section at the time! Had I caught the ghosts socializing, maybe even one moving the chair to sit down in it?

We left that area and followed him upstairs to the garret as usually, we would have already done that, and he didn't want to cheat us of the whole tour. There had been lights and other things seen here. One of the rooms up there always seemed to have a green light hovering inside it. Maybe it was the fireball from the past stories.

A funny story: they heard a noise from the attic space up there, so he had another investigator, Brad, check by going up to it and when Brad opened the door, squirrels scattered out of there. (The man at St. Luke's Church mentioned that there are those museum workers at Bacon's who don't like going into the attic, feeling some awful presence is up in the room).

Our guide pointed out that there had been writings and drawings on the wall made by children in the past. Not unlike kids today might take a marker and draw on the wall of their bedroom.

Done with that area and none of us having any experiences there, we followed him over to the Civil War side of the house. There was a door there with a WIFI camera facing it. They had caught things moving around inside the room it led into, and there had been no one in there. Also, the doorknob would move as if someone was turning it. He admitted to not being able to smell candles burning, and yet, he swore he breathed in the odor of burning candles in the room. To back him up, another investigator, Alan, who is a cop for the state, said he could smell the scent of candle wax melting. No candles are allowed to be burned in the building as it could burn down, and they don't have a sprinkler system because much of the place is original and water can ruin it.

Excerpt from Smith's Fort Plantation:

AUTHOR'S VISIT AND INVESTIGATION

Bill drove us to Smith's Fort Plantation by GPS. We almost missed the driveway, but we found it and drove up it to park near the house.

I did take the tour inside the house. The place was charming, and the guide knowledgeable. I even bought a couple of postcards.

I did a ghost box session and after that, an EVP one, to see what I could get, if anything, about any spirits lingering from Smith's Fort, the house and maybe even any natives. The tour guide had told me she doubted the place was haunted, unlike Preservation Virginia's other building in Surry, Bacon's Castle.

I did the ghost box first and turned it on.

"Any spirits still lingering here?"

A male voice uttered from the box, "Yes."

"Can you give me a name?" I said again, "A name."

No answer.

I asked again. A woman's voice said something, but it was low and static also muffled it.

I tried another question. "Did you come from Jamestown?"

A male voice said, "Yes."

Another voice said, "Virginia."

I asked how far from where I stood were the remains of Smith's second fort.

A different male voice said, "Three."

Three what? Yards? Feet? Miles? Not helpful.

"Are there spirits still haunting the house on this land?"

A male voice said, "Ghosts."

Another voice uttered, "Virginia."

I was excited as I heard the ghost and Virginia clearly and exclaimed, "Ghosts! Did you say ghosts?"

The male voice again replied, "Ghosts."

A female voice said, "Haunted Virginia."

Okay, that felt creepy to me. Virginia being said twice, the word, ghosts, too, and even more so, the woman using the phrase, Haunted Virginia.

I said thanks and shut off the box, doing a quick EVP session, but got nothing, except a cow mooing (as there were cows in the pasture next door) and a thump. The thump sounded close to me, and I cannot say for sure if that was paranormal.

I shut everything off and headed back to the car to hand all equipment to Bill before I went up to the house to take the tour. Afterward, I stopped by the field of flowers planted for butterflies that the tour guide told me about, took some pictures, and paid some money into a box for picking a couple of the flowers to take home. So many insects are disappearing with climate change, and it was great that someone was doing this.

AUTHOR'S VISIT AND INVESTIGATION
NOVEMBER 17, 2019

We returned on Sunday, November 17, 2019. It must have rained the night before as everything looked wet, and it was colder than the previous day, although the wind was not as bad. Many trees had taken on the costume of autumn, with various colors, and the gray, cloudy skies gave an aura of spookiness not there back in April. This time, the center was closed, so we couldn't stop there. We drove down the same road we had taken back in April, but we stopped at the sign that required us to purchase a permit to be allowed to drive our car down to Lake Drummond. Of course, not having enough change and no checks, I ended up doing a ghost box and EVP session there before taking some pictures.

I turned both the recorder and the ghost box on, setting the latter to scanning radio stations.

"Are there any spirits here in Dismal Swamp?"

"Who is connected to the Underground Railroad I see happened here? Anyone who became part of the maroon colony here?"

"Is the bride and her husband who'd been seen by a park ranger still haunting here? Any Colonial spirits here?"

"Philip," a male voice uttered from my ghost box.

A woman also replied, "Colton."

"First name?"

She said, "Fran."

Again, the male said, "Philip."

"How many spirits are here right now?"

A male voice said, "10."

But not actually hearing that at the time and thinking I heard nine, I asked if it was nine, and the same spirit said, "No!" (I heard all this better in the quiet of my home, off the laptop, and with headphones).

"Any ghost here connected to that slave rebellion that happened around here, where many white people were killed?"

A male voice uttered, "Bleed."

"Are any natives here, of local tribes?" I didn't get any answer to that, but again, this might be due to them not understanding English.

I attempted something else. "Have you seen pirates around here back when you were alive? Like Blackbeard?"

Nothing.

"Any ghosts here?"

A male voice said, "Yes." Then, I got, "John. Philip."

I said, "Dismal Swamp looks haunted to me."

What sounded like the same male voice replied, "It is."

"Anybody died here and is buried in the swamp?"

I got, "Three."

I said, "Goodbye. I'm leaving now, so don't follow me home, please. Good day."

A man called out from the box. "Goodbye."

I did a quick EVP session after I shut off the box. I asked several questions, but only one got me an EVP. I inquired if anyone had drowned in Lake Drummond and I did get "Lake Drummond."

We drove to the Washington Ditch Canal and drove down the road to the parking lot. I grabbed the ghost box and recorder and slung my camera around my neck, leaving Bill in the car.

I read the signs I saw there, taking pictures of them. One mentioned Washington Ditch and said: "Surveyed by George Washington in 1763. A cart road was built along this 4 ½ mile ditch, and the canal dug alongside by slave labor for transportation. Gresham Nimmo, under the personal direction of George Washington, did the surveying and kept the notes."

The other was about Dismal Town. It said, "Washington and company used this spot as their Dismal Swamp headquarters. The town was built prior to the Nimmo Survey of 1763 on Riddick 402 Acre Patent."

Now there is a word here that would come up three times in my ghost box session. At the time, I heard it and thought of the family who had it as their last name whose house was in Suffolk, but after listening to the recordings and looking at the picture, it was clear what the ghosts were trying to say.

I turned on both the ghost box and recorder, and I began.

"Any spirits here?"

Something answered but spoke too low.

"Names?"

"Riddick."

"Washington and company? George Washington?"

"Riddick." Second time for that word.

"Are there any spirits of slaves here? Connected to here or the swamp?"

A female voice from my box said, "Dug." (With slaves digging the canal, I understood later when I was home that this was a slave who dug the canal).

"Why are you still here?"

Something answered, but again too low.

"Do you feel you're stuck to this land?"

"Marked."

"Names?"

Once again, I got the word, "Riddick."

I said, "I am going now. Goodbye. Good day."

A male voice from my box uttered, "Good day."

I switched off the ghost box and the recorder, before hurrying back to the car. We still had two places in downtown historic Suffolk to investigate, and it was already 3:00 p.m. I needed to get home to eat and get all the audio and pictures uploaded.

The word Riddick came over three times through my ghost box, and it hit me what the spirits were telling me after looking at the sign in this photo.

Those who live in the area and tourists who visit claim they see wispy white things, especially around the lake, but no doubt what they saw could be foxfire, a substance given off when certain fungi decay wood. Again, maybe they did see something. The place can be eerie, especially if shrouded in fog or mist. And besides spirits, you might run into Bigfoot or fairies. Do take care and don't strike out alone in the woods and head off the designated trails, for you never know who or what you might meet. You might encounter more than animals and birds in the Great Dismal Swamp, and the haunts and Bigfoot are waiting to welcome you, even if it means taking the portal to Hell.

FROM
HANDBOOK FOR THE DEAD
"WORKING TO DEATH AND AFTER"
by Susan Schwartz

WORKING TO DEATH AND AFTER
Susan Schwartz

While winding down the old country back roads in Amelia County, Virginia, a charming family home can be found down beside a brick church. It is complete with farmland and a big red barn in the back. A mixture of animals seems apropos, including chickens, cows, dogs, and cats. It is a traditional working farm and home; however, it is home to many extra hands that don't realize they are no longer among the living.

The back door of the house has a tendency to open and close by itself, usually around 7pm every night. Apparently, Vernon, a previous owner, used to come home at that time after milking his cows. He also takes the time to remove his boots before entering the house. Walking through the back door and toward the kitchen, flashes of light twinkle down the hallway.

The kitchen seems to be a play land for the spirits. They love to rock any baskets that are hanging. Sometimes, one will swing while the other stays still. One Thanksgiving, one basket began to swing almost as if someone was pushing it. After the family had finished their dinner, the basket stopped swinging.

Upon entering into the living room, a large copy of the US Constitution hangs on the front wall. After taking a picture of it, the owners noticed a small face in one of the bottom corners that looked to be that of a Confederate soldier.

The bedroom next to the living room is where the owner's robe was found spread out on the bed after she laid it across the tub to retrieve something in the kitchen. When she returned, she found the robe had been moved to the bed. There was no one else present in the home.

In the hallway between the owner's bedroom and the next one, a little boy between the ages of seven and ten was seen peeking around the corners. After they closed off the hallway, they didn't see the little fellow again.

Off the kitchen, there is a dining area containing a table and some cabinets. The owners pulled up the carpet the summer before and found a bloodstain on the floor that looked exactly like a body had been lying there. They did some research and discovered a soldier had been stabbed to death in that very spot.

Bloodstain in the dining area

Going up to the second floor, there is a Victorian woman that resides at the top of the stairs, who doesn't like visitors. When visitors get to the third step, they will feel a hard push as if something is pushing them back down the stairs.

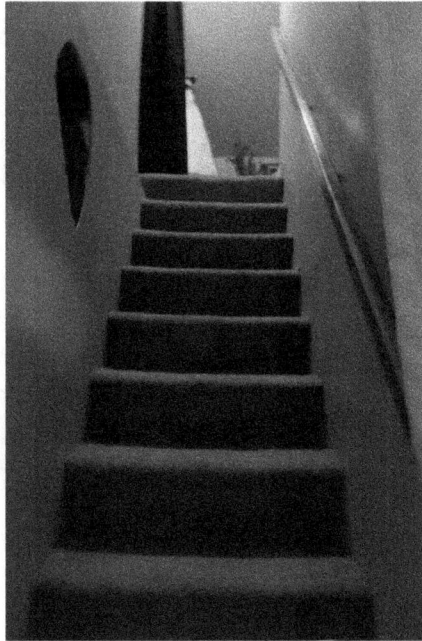
The stairs where people have been pushed

Many orb pictures have been taken in the attic area. Once enlarged, you can see faces in some of them. If you happen to be downstairs, you may even hear people walking around in the attic, even though the attic is always found empty.

Heading back downstairs, we stopped at a bathroom. The owner's daughter had never seen a ghost and didn't believe in them. One day, she came running out of the bathroom in quite a hurry. She noticed an orb coming to float right in front of her face for a moment, and then it left through the closed bathroom door. She stated she was now a believer.

Once outside, we explored the yard and barn area. There is a light seen across the field to the right of the house that comes almost every night. Looking like a lantern, the light moves toward the house, but halfway over, it disappears. A soldier's body was exhumed from the spot where the light disappears. Perhaps he is still guarding his land and keeping it safe.

Walking the path to the barn, the many animals follow you down the footpath. The barn has doors that open and close mysteriously by themselves. Could this be Vernon checking on his livestock?

Down below the barn in the trees, an old cemetery can almost be seen to the left, covered in branches and leaves. On the right, an old foundation from a house that used to stand there is peeking out. In addition, a midwife tended another house behind all of the graves. The front yard of that house was a burial ground for mothers and babies who died from childbirth in the 1800s.

FACTOIDS:

1.   The owners told me most of the research and stories that happened at their house the day I visited. They related many strange happenings throughout the tour, such as doors opening and closing, clothes being folded or laid out on the bed, and the sensation of being pushed back down the stairs while trying to get into the attic.

   a.   Vernon – The owner researched the house and discovered this gentleman's name as a former owner. They found out that he used to come in the back door at seven in the evening after tending to his cows. The barn doors also open and close by themselves. They thought it was Vernon tending to his animals.

   b.   The Bloodstain on the Floor – I was strongly pulled toward the kitchen door and kept asking the owner what was behind the door. Keep in mind, I had never been to the house before and didn't know what was in the dining room as the door was shut when I arrived. The owner's research led them to believe a man bled to death on the spot.

   c.   Victorian Woman – The owner has taken pictures showing a woman at the top of the stairs dressed in Victorian garb. About the time you reach the third step, you will feel a push as if she doesn't want you to come any further into her space. I felt a very strong push and had to grab the handrail to prevent myself from tumbling down the stairs.

   d.   The Bathroom Orb – This story was related to me by both owner's who thought their daughter had angered the ghosts by not believing. They reversed her opinion very quickly.

   e.   The Lantern in the Field – This light is seen on occasion crossing the field between the church and the house. It stops about halfway over and disappears. A soldier's body was exhumed from the very spot in the 1940s where the light fades out. The owner related a story where a soldier had just arrived at Fort Pickett with no way to get home. He hitched a ride with two other soldiers going the same way. They dropped him off a little before they arrived at their own home. They told him that he would need to walk the rest of the way. However, it being late, he walked back to the home of the two soldiers. Their father was a very mean man and told the soldier to leave the property or he would be shot. The soldier knocked on the door one more time, and the man shot him through the door. The family buried the body on their property. After the father died in the 1960s, the family could finally tell what happened that fateful night.

2. I felt many things while touring the home; I sometimes get pushes and pulls, and felt many of these that day. Pulled strongly to the kitchen door, I kept asking the owner what was behind it. Once the door opened, we saw the outline of the body. I was also pushed back down the steps while trying to enter the attic area. Grabbing the handrail saved me from tumbling back down the stairs.

3. Please see my write-up in my book, *Haunted Charlottesville and Surrounding Counties,* to read the full story and events.

4. The first picture is of the bloodstains; the second is of the stairs that I was pushed down.

ALSO AVAILABLE FROM FRIGHTENING FLOYDS PUBLISHING

MORE
MYSTERIOUS TALES
FROM
ANUBIS PRESS

AMERICAN CRYPTIC

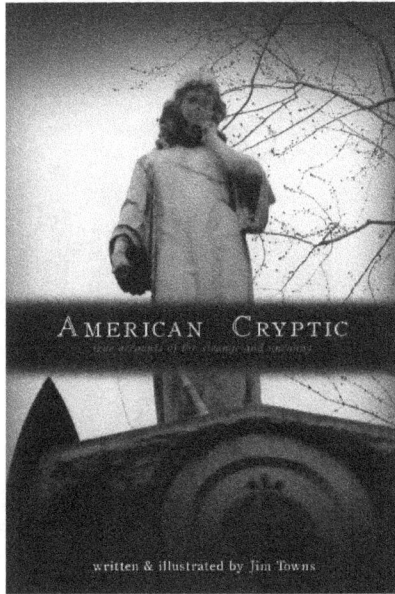

AMERICAN CRYPTIC is an open-minded cynic's take on the uncanny and sometimes frightening things which border our accepted reality. Through thirteen stories and essays, author and filmmaker Jim Towns examines several legends native to his own roots in Western Pennsylvania, and recalls some of his own unexplainable experiences as well. From legends of Native American giants buried under great earth mounds, to a haunted asylum, to a phantom trolley passenger, this work seeks not only to present the reader with new and fascinating supernatural tales, but also to deconstruct why our culture is so fascinated by their telling and re-telling.

HAUNTED SURRY TO SUFFOLK:
SPOOKY LOCATIONS ALONG ROUTES 10 AND 460

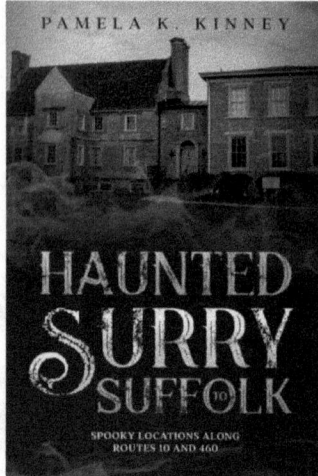

Take a journey along Virginia's scenic Routes 10 and 460 eastbound to enjoy the lovely countryside and metropolises that spread around these two roads. Most of all, discover that some historical houses, plantations, battlefields, parks, and even the modern cities, have more than touristy knickknacks, ham, and peanuts to offer. Many have ghosts!

Bacon's Castle has spirits haunting it since the 1600s. Stay in a cabin overnight at Chippokes Plantation State Park and you might find you have a spectral bedfellow. The city of Smithfield has more to offer than the world's oldest ham; it also has some very old phantoms still stalking its buildings. Take a ghost tour of Suffolk and see why the biggest little city is also one of the spookiest. Discover the myths and legends of the Great Dismal Swamp and see what phantoms are still haunting the wildlife refuge. And if that's not enough, Bigfoot and UFOs are part of the paranormal scenery. These and other areas of southeastern Virginia are teeming with ghosts, Sasquatch, UFOs, and monsters. See what awaits you along 460 south and 10. No matter which road you take, the phantoms can't wait to SCARE you a good time.

HANDBOOK FOR THE DEAD

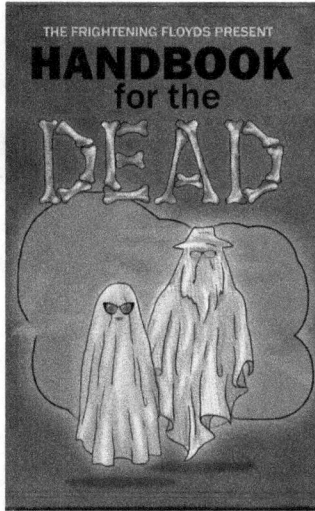

DON'T FORGET YOUR HANDBOOK...

Welcome all spirits! The Frightening Floyds present to you, *Handbook for the Dead* – a guide to help all new manifestations realize their functional perimeters.

Within this anthology, you'll read paranormal accounts from individuals who have experienced phantoms and disturbances that have not only chilled them, but also left them with some new insight into the supernatural. Now, they want to share their stories and wisdom with you. That way, if you're feeling a little flat, or even if you're a lost soul, you won't have to draw a door and knock.

Handbook for the Dead is sure to please the strange and unusual in everyone, and we promise it doesn't read like stereo instructions.

ALIENS OVER KENTUCKY

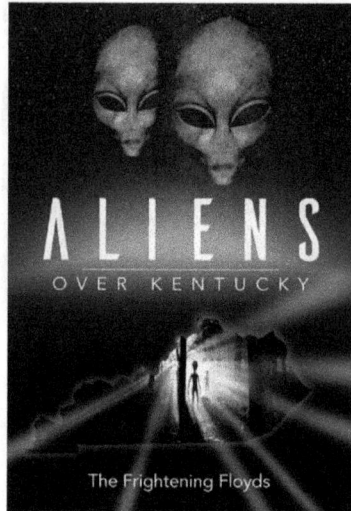

The Frightening Floyds

From the Frightening Floyds, the pair of paranormal enthusiasts who brought you *Be Our Ghost* and *Haunts of Hollywood Stars and Starlets* comes a new adventure into the realm of the unknown – *Aliens over Kentucky*.

This collection includes the most noted extraterrestrial encounters from the Bluegrass State, such as the Kelly Creatures Incident of 1955, the Stanford Abductions, the Dogfight above General Electric, and the tale of Capt. Thomas Mantell chasing a UFO through Kentucky skies. But that's not all. There are lesser known, but equally intriguing, reports herein, such as the train collision with the UFO, stories of unexplained crop circles and cattle mutilations, Spring-heeled Jack, the Meat Shower of 1876, and many eyewitness reports of various unidentified crafts. You'll also read a couple of personal experiences from the authors, and even Muhammad Ali gets involved in the alien action.

Join Jacob and Jenny Floyd as they dig into the mysterious cases and theories regarding Kentucky's "X-Files". Just be sure to keep one eye on the book and the other on the sky…

BE OUR GHOST

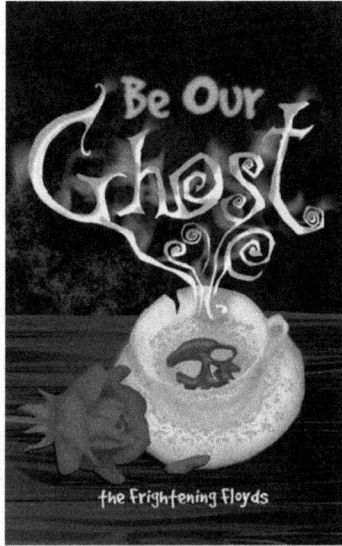

The Frightening Floyds invite you to be our ghost as we take you on a tour of the happiest haunted place on Earth! In this book, you will read about much of the alleged paranormal activity as well as urban legends spanning the various Disney theme parks around the world. From the haunted dolls of It's a Small World to the real ghosts of the Haunted Mansion, there are many spirits here to greet you. And make sure to say "Good morning" to George at Pirates of the Caribbean.

Enjoy the spooky and fascinating tales in *Be Our Ghost*! And don't worry, there are no hitchhiking ghosts ahead...or are there?

PARANORMAL ENCOUNTERS

The Frightening Floyds present *Paranormal Encounters*: a collection of 14 tales of true ghostly experiences. From a malevolent spirit remaining in an apartment, to a loving phone call from a lost relative; from a house with a sliding chair and slamming doors, to a snow globe moving across a bedroom; from a possible past-life experience to a ghostly stranger in a radio station, this anthology contains several strange and unusual stories that are sure to entertain fans of the paranormal.

HAUNTS OF HOLLYWOOD STARS AND STARLETS

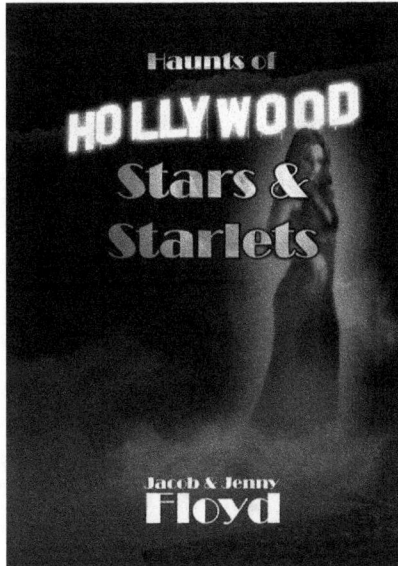

Explore the dark side of Tinseltown in this collection of paranormal stories, conspiracy theories, curses, and legends about some of Hollywood's most iconic names: Marilyn Monroe, Rudolph Valentino, Charlie Chaplin, James Dean, Jean Harlow, Clark and Carole, Lucille Ball, Michael Jackson, Bela Lugosi, Lon Cheney, John Belushi, and the King himself—Elvis Presley—and many more. Join the Frightening Floyds as they take you on a terrifying journey through the city of glamour and glitz!

FOR WESTERN
ADVENTURES
TRY
WILD WEST PRESS

BELLA

In an alternate 1800's America, where magic is real and dragons soar through the skies of the American frontier -

Topher had a good life, mostly. It wasn't great, but what can a young African girl expect living on the Edge of the World!

She had a shack that she shared with her Ma, she knew what vendors she could pocket an apple from, and was better than anyone with a spitshot. What more could a girl in the slums expect?

Then that chucklehead Wasco rolled out of the mountains like a toppled boulder. Topher had figured he might be good for a penny or two if she showed him around. Before she knew it he had her trompin' around the Blacklands, getting shot at, almost eaten and damn near gutted by some bull-headed dandy!

Jacob, who was about the handsomest gunfighter a body could imagine, might be some kind of monster. Old Ying turned out to be one of them wizards from the storybooks and Li had a magic sword!

All because someone went and took Bella and Wasco aimed to get her back, and Topher had been too stubborn not to follow him.

Yeah, it had been a good enough life. She just wasn't sure she was going to make it back to it, or if she even wanted to.

IF YOU LIKE HORROR,
STEP INTO THESE
TALES OF TERROR FROM
NIGHTMARE PRESS

THE GRAY MAN OF SMOKE AND SHADOWS

As a child, Hyeri's uncle tortured her. Years after escaping his brutal touch, she discovers a secret organization of vampires and joins the ranks of the undead. Gaining supernatural strength and speed, she seeks one thing: revenge.

When Hyeri unleashes her decades-old hatred upon her uncle, she's interrupted by a vampire enforcer who seeks to apprehend her for breaking company protocol and revealing her vampiric nature to mortals.

Hyeri fends off the assassin, but an errant attack wounds her uncle, and the vampires glimpse an evil that has taken refuge inside of him. The darkness desires to remain unknown and plots to silence them both.

Forced to combine their abilities, the vampire duo sharpen their swords and gorge on blood to increase their strength. Can they withstand the onslaught of Hyeri's uncle, *The Gray Man of Smoke and Shadows*?

Before they can find out, someone else stumbles onto their path. Someone with abilities they have never seen. This strange being, full of rage and vengeance, is hell-bent on destruction. But who will be his target?

Find out in Volume II of the Vampire Series of Extreme Horror based in South Korea.

BUTCHERS

Kidnapped, turned, and locked away in a concrete basement, high school student Sey-Mi is taught the ways of the damned. Her captors, beautiful and malignant, cruel and insane, torture her until she pledges allegiance to the *Gwanlyo*, a secret organization of vampires now obsessed with bringing her into their ranks.

Enter Cheol Yu and Hyeri, rogue members who want to liberate vampires and set them upon humankind like a plague. Their first act of rebellion is to persuade Sey-Mi to join them in their twisted objective of unraveling this draconian society of the dead. Before they can do that, they will have to dodge the Natural Police, an order within the *Gwanlyo* whose objective is to hunt down and butcher any vampires that break the organization's strict rules, and who are currently tracking Cheol Yu for murdering one of their own. Hyeri, who is no stranger to the organization's wicked methods of agonizing punishment, is hell-bent on bringing them down, and is prepared to lead Cheol Yu through the dark, abandoned streets of the *Gwanlyo*'s compound where Sey-Mi is being held captive. She doesn't intend to go in unarmed, however. Hyeri has a plan – one that might just burn the *Gwanlyo* to the ground.

Will Sey-Mi place her loyalties in the *Gwanlyo* that rules through terror? Will she side with rebellious conspirators who strive to bring hell to the world? Or will she carve out her own path through the flesh and bone of anyone who stands in her way?

Find out in *Butchers*, a novella of extreme horror.

CHAINSAW SISTERS

When Sis wakes up in her father's backyard, staring at a rickety old shed, she can't remember how she got there or even who she is. But she remembers Amy, the sister that disappeared long ago, the same sister that she now hears calling to her from the shed.

When Sis enters the shed she discovers that Amy is only there in spirit, and she is speaking to her through a new body, and that body just happens to be a chainsaw.

Amy reveals to Sis that she was murdered by a local crime ring and she needs Sis to seek revenge for her. Sis agrees to the task and as Amy guides her to the home of each man responsible, Sis uses Amy's new body to hack them to pieces.

But the situation isn't as straightforward as it seems. As Sis comes face to face with each man, she finds herself in the middle of unfamiliar flashbacks that put her at the scene of a heinous crime of which she has no recollection. In time, she begins to believe that these are not her memories and Amy isn't telling her everything she needs to know.

What lies ahead beyond the coming bloodbath is something darker and more disturbing than Sis could have imagined. Who is Amy? Who is Sis? And what connection do they both have to the men she's about to murder?

And why is her sister now a telepathic chainsaw?

Also includes three short stories about a demonic hollow, killer pizzas, and space zombies.

ANIMAL UPRISING!

A lion, a hybrid, a bear – oh no! A goat, a gull, and a big black dog! Can't forget the roaches, the deer flies, and the tarantula hawk, or the abominable insect that rises from the earth! We got creepy crawlers and killer critters for everyone. Oh, you want mythical creatures? How about a malevolent spirit posed as a fox, a rambunctious jackalope, or a herd of unicorn-gazelles on a distant planet? Let's not forget the supernatural silver stag with the power to raise the dead. Oh, did I mention the giant mantis shrimp? Yeah – we got a giant mantis shrimp. Humankind really has their work cut out for them in this collection of terrifying tales of beastly butchery. Need to know more? Check out *Animal Uprising!* for all of the mayhem.

NIGHT OF THE POSSUMS

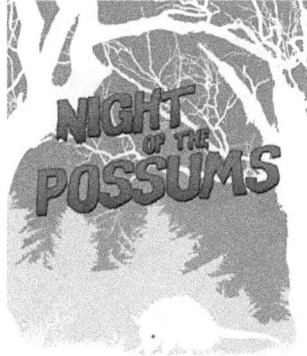

JACOB FLOYD

The night of the possums began on a chilly autumn morning around 2am in late October.

On a dark country road, a young man is torn to shreds by wild animals. The news of his grisly death rocks the town. When a similar death occurs later that day, the town is in the grips of fear.

In rural Bardstown, Kentucky, opossums have risen up against the populace. People are being maimed and devoured throughout the city. These are not your ordinary opossums, either: they are smarter, stronger, faster, and far more vicious—some larger than any opossum anyone has ever seen, growing as long as four feet and as heavy as fifty pounds, with teeth capable of cleaving bone.

As the flesh-eating scourge quickly spreads from one end of Bardstown to the other, a few of those who survived the attacks band together in an attempt to eradicate the maniac marsupials. But, the number of the beasts grows by the hour and the force becomes too insurmountable and the survivors soon realize escape is their only option.

But, beyond the berserk behavior of the carnivorous creatures is a darker secret—something ancient and unnatural that threatens all those who are bitten. Before anyone can find out what is driving these opossums to kill, the survivors must battle their way through the merciless onslaught of claws and teeth and leave the threat of Bardstown behind them.

POETRY FANS,
CHECK OUT
POET TREE GROVE

MAN IN THE SHADOW LAND

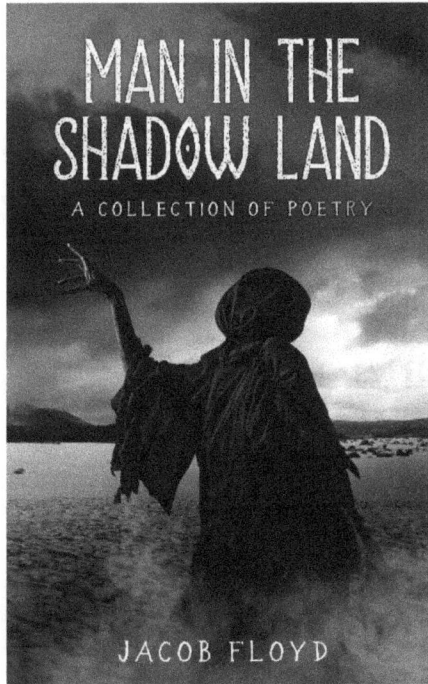

Welcome to the Shadow Land…

In this book, you will find poems about death, sorrow, madness, fear, and other aspects of life that haunt the Man in the Shadow Land. This collection spans ten years of the author's life, and contains some of his most authentic pieces. From his Poe-inspired poetry to those written from the darkest places of his heart, *Man in the Shadow Land* is a journey into a soul full of shadowy corners.

COMING SOON:

FROM ANUBIS PRESS:

Haunted Hotels of Virginia
Susan Schwartz

Kentucky's Strange and Unusual Haunts
The Frightening Floyds

Werewolves and Other Shapeshifters Stalking America
Pamela K. Kinney

FROM NIGHTMARE PRESS:

Retro Horror
An anthology

The Cursed Diary of a Brooklyn Dog Walker
Michael Reyes

The Untaken
Bekki Pate

All Roads Lead
Jennifer Winters

Viva La Muerte
Quinn Hernandez

Whoops! I Woke the Dead
Joseph Rubas

In Dormancy, They Sleep
D.G. Sutter

The Woodshed
Jacob Floyd

FROM WILD WEST PRESS

The Dark Frontier
An anthology

Thank you for reading! If you like the book, please leave a review on Amazon and Goodreads. Reviews help authors and publishers spread the word!

To keep up with more Anubis Press news, join the Anubis Press Dynasty on Facebook.

www.ingramcontent.com/pod-product-compliance
Lightning Source LLC
Chambersburg PA
CBHW050133280326
41933CB00010B/1356